SURVIVORS OF THE ARMADA

Donne: A Spirit in Conflict

Swift: The Conjured Spirit

Swift: Selected Prose Writings (edited)

Thomas Hardy, A Critical Biography

Thomas Hardy's Notebooks (edited)

Some Recollections, by Emma Hardy
    (edited with Robert Gittings)

Summer in another World

SPANISH MARINER'S ASTROLABE (1585)
Found off Valencia Island, Co. Kerry (1845)

SURVIVORS
OF
THE ARMADA

EVELYN HARDY

CONSTABLE

LONDON

Published by Constable and Company Ltd
10–12 Orange Street, London WC2

© Evelyn Hardy 1966

First published 1966

Printed in England by
C. Tinling & Co. Ltd.
Liverpool, London and Prescot

Contents

Illustrations

To
the memory
of
GARRETT
MATTINGLY

ADVICE GIVEN BY THE PURSER-IN-CHIEF TO THE *ARMADA* IN A COUNCIL OF WAR HELD ON BOARD THE *SAN MARTÍN* WHEN ENTERING THE NORTH SEA ON TUESDAY, 'THE EVE OF SAN LORENZO' (AUGUST 9th) 1588

It was resolved that the Armada should set its course for Spain. Captain Alonso de Benavides and Captain Vasco de Carbajal asked Purser Calderon what course that was; to which he replied that *it would be a tremendously laborious one, for we should have to sail round England, Scotland, and Ireland, 750 leagues, through stormy seas almost unknown to us,* before we could reach Coruña. He then took careful stock of the bread and water on board—for everything else was lacking . . .

Pedro Coco Calderon.[1]

---

[1] C.S.P.S., p. 447, from the *Statement of the Events which happened to the Royal Armada, commanded by the Duke of Medina Sidonia, from the time it left Coruña, where it had taken refuge from the gales it encountered after it sailed from Lisbon,* dated September 24th, 1588. (Italics mine.)

SAILING ORDERS "FOR THE RETURN OF THE ARMY INTO SPAIN" GIVEN OUT OFF ROCKALL BY THE DUKE OF MEDINA SIDONIA TO THE FLEET

The course that is first to be held is to the north-north-east, until you be found under 61 degrees-and-a-half; and then to take great heed lest you fall upon the Island of Ireland, for fear of the harm that may happen unto you upon that coast.

Then parting from those Islands, and doubling the Cape in 61 degrees-and-a-half, you shall run west-south-west until you be found under 58 degrees; and from thence to the south-west to the height of 53 degrees; and then to the south-south-west, making to the Cape Finisterre, and so to procure your entrance into the Groyne (Coruña) or to Ferol, or to any other port of the coast of Galicia.[1]

---

[1] Undated Quarter sheet. C.S.P.I., pp. 49–50. Forwarded by Lord Deputy Fitzwylliam to Lord Burghley from Dublin Castle on October 1/10th, 1588. Said to have been found and taken from one of the wrecked vessels in Ireland. The course was not adhered to by many of the ships. Spotswood-Green states that "there is an error of transcription in the last 'leg' of this course. It should read SE and *not* SSW. The Spanish words for *east* and *west* are so alike the error was easy" (p. 434).

Acknowledgments

All writers on the Armada owe a special debt of gratitude to Garrett Mattingly, whose splendid dramatic narrative work was the first of its kind to be written or published in nearly four hundred years with a single minor exception. I acknowledge mine gladly. But since he covered the ramifications of the entire European background it was impossible for him to do little more than mention the involvement of Ireland and the wrecks off the Irish coasts, and it is on these that I have concentrated. While indebted to him for short quotations (as well as to his publishers, Messrs. Jonathan Cape and Houghton Mifflin, and to Mrs. Mattingley for their use), I have taken it for granted that readers are familiar with his *Defeat of the Spanish Armada* and with Chapter XXI entitled "The Long Road Home".

I have myself preferred to draw mainly on the Calendars of State Papers for the period for the bulk of my information: but I wish to acknowledge information courteously rendered me by the Director of the Archivo General de Simancas; the National Maritime Museum, Greenwich; the National Museum of Ireland, and the Metereological Office, Dublin; the British Museum, the Ashmolean, and the County Museum, Armagh.

I am indebted also to the Royal Geographical Society for allowing me to quote extensively from the Reverend Spotswood Green's address, reprinted in the *Geographical Society Journal,* and to reproduce his accompanying Map of the Wrecks: likewise the Royal Irish Academy for permission to quote from the same author's article on the Kerry wrecks, and from Mr. Purser's translation of Paymaster Aramburu's account of his ship's adventures off the Blasket Islands, published in the Academy's *Proceedings*.

The following have also granted permission to quote from their authors: the Council of the Navy Records Society, Penguin Books, and Messrs. J. M. Dent. The Spanish and Irish Tourist Boards have also been helpful, the latter generously providing their photographs free of charge. The Staff of the London Library has been, as always, unfailingly attentive.

Finally, it is with pleasure that I thank Frances Partridge for her vivid translation of Captain de Cuellar's narrative *Letter*; my friend, Esme Strachey, for helping with proofs; and Sheila Beringer for her patience in unravelling a difficult hand and the complexities of many footnotes.

Main Sources

Title	Footnote abbreviation
Calendar of the State Papers relating to Ireland of the Reign of Elizabeth, preserved in Her Majesty's Public Record Office, August 1588–September 1592. Edited by Hans Claude Hamilton (London, 1885).	C.S.P.I.
Calendar of Letters and State Papers relating to English Affairs, preserved in, or originally belonging to the *Archives of Simancas*, Vol. IV, Elizabeth, 1587–1603, edited by (Sir) Martin A. S. Hume (London, 1899).	C.S.P.S.
La Armada Invencible, C. Fernandez Duro (Madrid, 1885), 2 Vols.	DURO
State Papers relating to the Defeat of the Spanish Armada, (Sir) John Knox Laughton (Navy Records Society, 1895), 2 Vols.	LAUGHTON
Armada Ships on the Kerry Coast, Rev. William Spotswood-Green, Proceedings of the Royal Irish Academy, Vol. XXVII, Sec. C., (Dublin and London 1908–9): including a translation of part of Paymaster Marcos de Aramburu's Account.	ARAMBURU
Captain Cuellar's Adventures in Connacht and Ulster, A.D. 1588, Hugh Allingham, to which	A/C

is added An Introduction and Translation of
Captain Cuellar's Narrative of the Spanish
Armada and his Adventures in Ireland; Robert
Crawford (London, 1897).

Remarks on Certain Passages in Captain Cuellar's   O'REILLY
Narrative of His Adventures in Ireland after the
wreck of the Spanish Armada in 1588–9, fol-
lowed by a literal Translation of that Narrative;
Professor A. J. P. O'Reilly, Proceedings of the
Royal Irish Academy, Vol. III, 3rd Series
(Dublin, 1893–6).

The Defeat of the Spanish Armada, Garrett Mat-   MATTINGLY
tingly (Jonathan Cape, London, 1959).

The Wrecks of the Spanish Armada on the Coast of   SPOTSWOOD-
Ireland, W. Spotswood-Green, Geographical   GREEN
Journal, May, 1906, Vol. XXVII, No. 5.

I

Destination of the Fleet:
Links between Ireland and Spain:
The Religious Question

ON May 9th, 1588, the *Spanish Armada*, which was never officially called *Invincible* in Spain but rather the *Grand* or *Felicitous Fleet*, set sail from Lisbon. The word *Invincible* which has echoed with mocking irony down the centuries

> probably sprang out of the idle talk of some of the young adventurers, braggarts as became their age, or out of the silly gossip of the Lisbon taverns.[1]

On May 28th the great ships began to move up the Tagus and warp out of harbour, having been thwarted in their attempts to make progress by the wintry-wild weather; and by May 30th the whole Armada was standing out to sea. The fleet's destination, strictly commanded by the Duke of Medina Sidonia, was first the "Scilly Isles, and ships must try to sight the islands from the south", and secondly "Mount's Bay, St. Michael's, between Cape Longnose [Land's End] and the Lizard".[2] But again, in weather which the Duke wrote to King Philip was more like December than May, contrary winds kept the fleet beating backwards and forwards, or scuttling for safe harbourage, until on June 19th the main body of ships was forced to put into Coruña, where officers and men assessed the storm's damage and set about refitting and revictualling. On July 22nd, more than ten weeks after their initial sailing, the Armada again set sail, with a good south wind, only to be maddeningly becalmed at sea. But by the 30th the

---

[1] Laughton I, pp. xxix–xxx.
[2] C.S.P.S., pp. 291–2.

Fleet Flagship, Santa Cruz's *San Martín*, had sighted the Lizard.

Among those attached in a humble way to this expeditionary force was one Nicholas Furlong, an Irishman, "who lay at the Groyne [Coruña] when the Spanish Fleet departed" and was later wrecked with his ship off the west coast of his native country. Under examination he declared that from Coruña the Armada had departed with close on

> *22,000* men to land at Mount's Bay: the Duke of Parma to land in the Isle of Wight with 40,000: the Duke de Guise with 20,000: the King of Scots to invade the North of England with 30,000:

and for good measure he added to all these round thousands that there were with the fleet "500 English and Irish with the Spanish army".[1]

It would be easy to state that Furlong's figures were inflated— and here we are concerned only with his first figure, the men with the fleet—and that no such vast force *could* be carried on the ships' decks, leaving out of account the huge land forces. But examination of the *Statement of the Ships and men of all ranks and conditions present at the muster at Coruña on the 13th of July, held on the Royal Armada under the command of the Duke of Medina Sidonia, etc.*[2] (hereafter called the Coruña Muster), gives a grand total of 27,000 and four men, omitting 450 men in hospital on shore but including 1,549 who were still tossing about at sea between the Scillies and Coruña, having been prevented from getting together with the fleet as commanded. When this total is taken into account it is not surprising that fear seeped into the minds of men both in England and Ireland as the Armada approached the shores of the former and was wrecked on the coasts of the latter. No such gigantic force had ever been known to put aboard in the history of the world. Could the English navy hope to outwit it as it sailed up Channel? Could the Irish be trusted not to be won over later to the side of the Spaniards? And indeed this was the

[1] C.S.P.I., pp. 27–8.
[2] C.S.P.S., pp. 339–42.

doubt in the minds of Lord Deputy Fitzwylliam and the Council of Ireland when he forwarded Furlong's *Examination* on September 9/19th from Dublin to Treasurer Burghley, and wrote:

> there are here seducing spirits that cease not to abuse the expectation of this country people with rumours contrary.[1]

Furlong's account was given proof of veracity when he disclosed his sources—a master-gunner in the Spanish navy, one Patrick Lynch, another Irishman, who in turn got his information from his ship's Captain. A third supply-source was a Jesuit priest called Rochford who had died at the Groyne.

But there was more to come from this startling examination, for Furlong declared that:

> the Spanish army *would have sailed for Ireland* if it had been delayed a fortnight later at the Groyne and would, in that case, have entered Waterford [on the east coast] and Beare Haven [on the west coast] there to winter and abide until the next spring.[2]

Such a statement may have been mere wishful thinking on the part of the three Irishmen, homesick for their green fields like the dying Falstaff, hoping perhaps to desert when they reached home ports. We shall never know now whether there was any foundation stone of truth in the declaration. No entry either in the *State Papers Spanish*, or *Ireland*, provides any official corroboration, nor, as far as I know, does any extractor of records, like Duro, Laughton and Mattingly, or any writer on the Armada up to date. But the picture of the Grand Fleet riding at anchor in Irish harbours as snug as mergansers entirely leaves out of account what Drake, Hawkins and Lord Howard of Effingham might have done. The contingency would have been one to fire Drake's explosive heart and imagination.

Except by word of mouth exchanged between traders, merchants and fishermen who were familiar with Irish ports little was known by the Spaniards of the interior of Ireland, little of the landscape, and nothing of the Irish country-folk and their way of

[1] & [2] C.S.P.I., p. 27 and p. xvi. (Italics mine.)

life. To our survivor and writer-in-chief, de Cuellar, the people seemed barbarous and savage. They were so to the English who with the patronage of a more powerful invading race were ignorant of, and uninterested in Ireland's glorious past, of her Gaelic customs, laws, legends, language and literature; her caste of Catholic thought in a religion which they had once shared; or her methods of intricate skilled warfare adapted to the difficult terrain—never fully-mastered by any invading soldier, no matter how experienced he had become in continental warfare.

Tudor England with her growing population and increased vitality sought expansion to the west, at the same time attempting to ward off the thrust of a Spain enriched with the gold of Peru whose sovereign, in addition to his native country, ruled over the Netherlands, Southern Italy and Sicily, Sardinia, Milan, the Spanish colonies in the Americas and (after 1590) Portugal and all the Spanish colonies in the Indies. Ireland's involvement in her neighbour, England's, problems was inevitable, yet her position, not only geographically, was ambiguous. Close to English and continental shores she was yet remote and detached: small in size she was of great importance to a stronger power who could use her as a base or an ally against England. By 1588, misunderstood and mishandled by successive English sovereigns and governments, decimated by meaningless bitter wars, and rebellious under increasing religious tyranny, both oppressed and depressed, she had become wholly unfit to meet the impact of a new Renaissance world from whose influences she had remained virtually untouched, or to become involved in what Mattingly calls "the first great international crisis in modern history". In this state of mental bewilderment and despair she was increasingly drawn to Rome, or to Spain, for understanding and practical support. Since the three countries shared the same form of Christian faith this was natural, but the links with Spain were far more numerous and ancient, more subtly forged than those with Italy. They were, and are, geological, botanical, ethnological, archaeological, historical and commercial, even in one basic instance linguistic. Here we are concerned only with the racial and commercial, as they impinge on questions pertinent to the hurling of the Spaniards on Irish shores in the autumn of 1588.

There is a common supposition that large, undefined numbers of Irishmen and women are descended from survivors of the Armada, a theory that Mattingly succinctly disposes of in fourteen lines. Anyone who studies the State Papers and other contemporary accounts of events in that terrible year must come to the same conclusion—that it is improbable that the few "ragges of men", as Lord Deputy Fitzwylliam described the starved, shipwrecked, emaciated, half-dying Spaniards who were washed up and remained alive, should beget numerous descendants. Either they died like flies on landing, or they were exterminated at once on strands, rocks and shoals, or later in bogs, woods and mountains in which they had taken refuge; in camps, prisons or market squares. We have an example of the first in the young soldier, who had fought at Terceira, who died beside the sleeping de Cuellar during the night.

The men of rank who were saved from the sword for ransom were kept close confined in castles in the west or north, until they could be conveyed to those in the east for easier transport to England. The common soldiers or sailors who survived and were sheltered by friendly chieftains got away through Irish or Scottish aid as quickly as they could, to Scotland or the continent, their overpowering instinct being to escape the English whom they observed slaughtering their companions, harrying the Irish and hounding themselves. An inconsequential number, as we shall see, remained in service in the north with that Prince of Elizabethan Irishmen, the Great O'Neill, but these were an exception. Any physical similarities of the Irish to the Spanish may therefore more reasonably be attributed to their common Iberian blood and the intermingling of the two races throughout many centuries past, facilitated by trade and commerce.

The commercial links between Ireland and Spain, fostered by the prevailing south-westerly winds, appear to go back to Mesolithic times. Here archaeology confirms ethnology. During the

Bronze Age Irish gold attracted Spanish seekers, and shoals of fish of astonishing proportions drew Spanish fishermen, as they do today in diminished numbers, especially in the west where one may see Spanish trawlers tied up at the quays of Killybegs, Galway, Bantry and smaller harbours, the men being familiarly called "Spanners".

Trade between Ireland and Spain flourished in the reign of Elizabeth. In 1572 Sir Humphrey Gilbert, given charge of Munster in 1569, made a report to the Queen in which he listed as many as 600 Spanish fishing-smacks, and stressed the permanent fishing establishments along the coasts. Sir Francis Drake and Sir John Hawkins later drew up a scheme for capturing both trading and fishing boats.[1] It took a Hawkins or a Drake to read the potential danger in such numbers of Spanish vessels in Irish waters during a time of war. But list and scheme alike appear to have been ignored as impracticable.

At this time Ireland's chief ports were Dublin, Drogheda, Waterford and Cork in the east and south; and Limerick, Galway, Killybegs and Dingle in the west. Galway and Dingle have always been harbours favoured by the Spaniards. In 1589 Galway was stated to be "unapt to withstand a regular siege" because of the mountains that lie round about it. In the spring of 1591-2 Sir Richard Byngham, that "flail of Connacht" whose name appears frequently in later pages, strongly advised that:

> Galway being an open road [stead], and a town inhabited by a people that do generally favour the Spanish nation and their religion, their merchants having intercourse and daily traffic with the Spaniards, there is great likelihood that the enemy should as soon bend his force for that place as for any other city or town within this realm [Ireland]. And that town is the worst provided for, and furnished of means to defend the same of all the towns in Ireland, for there is not so much as a gunner there, a piece of artillery . . . mounted, or any munition for war.[2]

[1] *Carew Papers*, 1572, p. 422; and 1580, pp. 285-6, Also C.S.P.S., p. 20.
[2] C.S.P.I., p. 470.

In the same year he warned the Council that "merchants of Galway do daily come out of Spain", and reminded Burghley that he had advised him two years ago that the garrison should be strengthened with men sent out of England. Byngham was an old campaigner who had served *with* the Spaniards at St. Quentin in 1557, and Lepanto (against the Turks) in 1571–2: he then fought *against* them in the Low Countries as a volunteer with the Dutch. After service against Desmond in Ireland he became Captain of the *Swiftsure* involved in the massacre at Smerwick or *Dun an Oir*; was knighted in 1584 and appointed Governor of Connacht, an office which he held almost uninterruptedly until his death in 1599. His conduct towards both Spanish and Irish was savage and merciless. He was, however, conversant with the province which he governed and it is curious that his advice about Galway's vulnerability was never heeded, the explanation being perhaps that, in spite of recurrent rumours that Philip was arming again, the scene of danger in Ireland, in the decade following the Armada, had shifted from the west to her northern and southern shores.

Dingle town and Dingle Bay, which appear prominently in the *State Papers Domestic* when concerned with the Armada ships off the Blasket Islands, are of especial importance when considering the Hispano-Irish trading links. Long before the ships' arrival Dingle, the most westerly walled town in Europe, was favoured by princely Spanish merchants, whose tall imposing stone houses were the admiration of the humbler native inhabitants. Spaniards are said to have played an active part in the social, religious, civic and industrial life of the community, and the old church whose patron saint is St. James—an unusual dedication in the west of Ireland but common in Spain, where he is the patron saint of the nation—is believed to have been erected through the generosity of the Spanish residents.[1]

In this trade lay the danger which Gilbert and Drake had foreseen, for on Spanish and Irish merchants' ships unapprehended spies might voyage; friars or priests disguised as servants or

[1] *History of Kerry*, Dr. Charles Smith, 1756.

students might readily contact such inaccessible figures as Philip of Spain or the Pope. English restrictions were therefore placed on trade and the export of certain commodities was strictly prohibited. Even the Auditor of Ireland, Christopher Peyton, was forced to write despairingly to Burghley that goods sent to his son "at board" near Rochelle—barrels of beef, butter, candles and tallow, "about a ton in all", and a small "cask of apparel" had been seized "to the Queen's use" and an indictment of felony brought against him.[1] Yet the small ships from Ireland sometimes got through since it was not possible to enforce embargoes so strictly in the west as in the Irish and English Channels.

Another danger for the English was that Spanish ships might put into Irish harbours to victual, or send out victuals to Spain or Portugal. One witness testifies that "the men of Waterford were always forward to help" the Spaniards, stating that they had recently taken out to Lisbon, for the fleet when it was preparing to sail, "1,000 pecks of corn and half a score [of] horses".[2]

Among the crews of the Armada ships it is possible that there was a large number of men accustomed to take part in the Irish fishery or other trades. But apart from Captain Fernandez Duro's list of pilots with the fleet, and the revealing examinations of prisoners on Irish soil, we have small proof of this. We know little of the sailors with the Armada (despised by the soldiers who were double their number), some of them galley-slaves, some pressed into service, some seasoned nautical officers whose position alongisde the military was uncomfortable and delicate.

That there were Irish refugees driven out of their country by religious or other persecution among the soldiers and sailors of the fleet, avid for employment, pay and adventure, is likely. We hear of several—James Machary of Tipperary, and William Browne of Waterford, aged 23, who give evidence in the State Papers, and the three Irishmen mentioned in the opening pages.

[1] C.S.P.I., p. 125.
[2] Ibid., p. 67. The *C.S.P. Spanish* give details of contraband Scottish trade with Spain, and cargoes of Spanish delicacies for London shipped as "decoys" for Spanish merchant-spies.

We have proof of Irish bishops, priests, friars and monks passing between Ireland and Spain before, during, and after 1588, constantly referred to as dangerous and suspect persons by the English reporters: and the Armada lists give as many as 180 monks and friars and four priests accompanying the fleet, some of them Irish and a few possibly Scottish and English as well.

The presence of priests, monks and friars brings us to the religious element which became an integral part of England's Irish wars, the dropcloth behind Captain de Cuellar's, and his companions' and protectors' actions. As far as England was concerned the wars with Ireland were not exclusively religious in their origins. During the revival of interest in Ireland in the reign of Henry VIII they savoured more of expansion and colonization, seasoned with the spirit of adventuring.

Ironically, it was not until the reign of a Catholic Queen, Mary, that the

> psychological infiltration was accompanied by anything serious in the way of conquest by force:[1]

and not until the reign of her sister, Elizabeth, did the serious wars of conquest begin. Mattingly has stressed that the coming of the Armada was part of an ideological war—

> a final struggle to the death between the forces of light and the forces of darkness . . . upon its outcome was felt to hang . . . the fate . . . of all Christendom. Ideological wars are revolutionary wars, easily transcending national boundaries, and always, at least in intention and in the imaginations of the men involved in them, total wars.[2]

Chadwick reiterates this in another way:

> The wars of religion were only about religion in a restricted sense. . . . None of the great expeditions, not even the Spanish Armada against England, was a crusading expedition in the idealistic sense of Pope Urban the II's crusade against the Holy Land . . .

[1] *The Story of Ireland*, Sean O'Faolain, London, 1943, p. 22.
[2] p. 15.

But

the religious motive was the most compelling motive in the minds of individuals or groups.[1]

From 1569 onwards James Fitzmaurice Fitzgerald and his line had been marked out for English destruction because of the Desmond risings and Rebellions. When Don Alonso de Luzon (who appears obliquely in de Cuellar's *Letter*), prisoner in the grim castle at Drogheda, was examined, one of the questions that the Lord Deputy stipulated should be put to him was:

Item 10: To know whether James Fitzmaurice's son came out of Spain; if he did, in what ship, and what became of him.[2]

To which Don Alonso replied on October 13/23rd that he knew nothing of any such man. Yet the son, Maurice Fitzgerald, who had been in Spain, was indeed with the Armada, apparently on the *Duquesa Santa Ana*, since it is recorded that he died of a fever on board ship and "was cast into the sea with great solemnity before Torane".[3]

By 1588 the wars had become closely identified with the expansion of Protestantism on one side and with the protection of the old faith on the other. But one cannot force the image of a cruel, more powerful invader tyrannically suppressing a spirited and united, but backward country into subservience. Ireland was far from unified, or free from personal rivalries among her chieftains. This lack of unity made it hard and dangerous for her when she became the battleground for a complex of international ideologies, as well as rival personal ambitions, to be fought out on her blood-soaked land. Captain de Cuellar affords abundant evidence of such disunity among the chieftains, some of whom had thrown in their lot with the more powerful English, and others who held fast to the ancient Gaelic concepts of loyalty, service, protection of their lands, cattle and people, even though

[1] *The Reformation*, Owen Chadwick, Penguin Books, 1964, pp. 365–6.
[2] Laughton II, pp. 270, 275.
[3] C.S.P.I., pp. 47, 63, 65.

this courted death by musket-shot in bog, lake or mountain, or public execution in Ireland or London.

In April of Armada year the tension between his Holiness Pope Sixtus V and Philip II of Spain was heightened by the launching of the huge Enterprise, in which Sixtus had always expressed acute interest since he himself had urged Philip on from the first year of his papacy. It was known that he had promised to *give*, not lend, the King, a million golden ducats on the day that the first Spanish soldier set foot on English soil. And now it looked as though Philip's megalomaniac scheme might materialize, and victory ensue.

Meanwhile Philip, "in a sense a junior partner with Providence", with a fanatical belief in his divinely directed powers, sat weaving his complex web in the fastness of the Escurial. Working as we should say today "by remote control", and lacking those modern inventions which might have ensured that all that he had envisaged, striven for, and commanded might be carried out, he declared that his motive for attempting to invade England arose "from a religious motive only, and not for a desire for new kingdoms". Indeed it was common knowledge that he had vowed that

> this was to be the last enterprise he will undertake in his life, and he has determined to offer it to God, for his service, and the exaltation of the Catholic faith.[1]

It is possible to delude oneself, even in religious matters, and if historians have accused Elizabeth, James, Parma, and other protagonists in this European drama, of duplicity surely we may accuse Philip of self-deception. Whatever his declared motive and whatever his statements Elizabeth, her ministers, officers and citizens, could not be expected to interpret his actions in any other light than a determination to hold England as a semi-dependency.

---

[1] C.S.P.S., pp. 263–6.

2

Causes for the Armada's Destruction off Ireland: The Factor of the Weather

"The wrecks in Ireland and round Scotland account for all the fighting ships of the Armada lost, except to enemy action",[1] writes Garrett Mattingly, adding that forty-four of this class remained out of sixty-eight on September 3rd. On this day, eleven days before the first recorded Spanish wreck on the Irish shores, Medina Sidonia wrote off to the King from latitude 58° north:

> the wind has now veered . . . but the winds on this coast are always more tempestuous than elsewhere.[2]

In spite of the tendency today to minimize the importance of the gales off the western and northern coasts of Ireland during the autumn of 1588, local weather conditions, according to survivors' reports, played (as we shall see) a decisive part in the destruction of this large number of the fighting ships.

But there were other causes. In fact the causes working for defeat and destruction were in large measure the same, with the exception of the signal superiority of the English "new warfare", about which Philip had known when *preparing* the fleet, and which Medina Sidonia gallingly confirmed off Achill Head on August 21st, long after the battles up-Channel. Only, as the battered ships fled into the North Sea, rounded the Scottish coasts, threaded the islands, and bore down on Ireland and the fleet divided in the gales—some coming in too close to shore attempting to escape destruction while others standing out to sea made their mournful way homeward—these were intensified.

[1] p. 311.
[2] C.S.P.S., pp. 411–12.

Chief among them was the dissension prevailing between the Spanish officers. In his selection of Medina Sidonia as Commander in Chief, an appointment the Duke regarded with dismay and tried to refuse, Philip had thought to please both the military and naval commanders of the Armada. But in this combined enterprise, in which there were double the number of soldiers to sailors, the military officers were jealous of each other's prowess and reputation, and the naval restive under traditional military control and a belief in its superiority. A magnificent seaman like Admiral de Recalde was precluded from being given superior command because of tradition. Since the "flower of the Spanish nobility" and army were to accompany the Armada, no seaman, no matter how brilliant or experienced, could take precedence over them, whilst the sailors would not be subservient and obedient to a military officer unless he should be of the highest rank. This maintaining of traditional precedence lay like a dead hand on the vast enterprise, dooming it if not to disaster at least to a difficult and uneasy command. We have proof of the jealousies and rivalries among the Spanish officers without going to the State Papers in Captain de Cuellar's narrative. When describing his own escape from hanging at the yard-arm he says:

> The Duke was in retirement [in his cabin], and very morose, and unwilling that anyone should speak with him . . . and the councillors, to make up for his perversity, did wrongs right and left, on the lives and reputations of blameless persons; and this is so public that every one knows it.

Another contributory cause for destruction was the tall top-heavy masts—often made of oak and sometimes, like the *San Salvador*'s, clamped together. We know that the towering masts amazed and awed the English, among them some fishermen from Southampton who encountered the Spanish fleet near the Orkneys; and when Lord Deputy Fitzwylliam made his late, winter journey in 1588 to the northern and western coasts, after most of the doomed ships had already been wrecked, he exclaimed in astonishment at the timber lying strewn over a single wide strand, Streedagh, on which de Cuellar's companions perished—

> more than would have built five of the greatest ships that ever I saw, besides mighty great boats, cables and other cordage . . . and some such masts for bigness and length, as in mine own judgement I never saw any two could make the like.[1]

Masts were, in fact, already giving trouble off Cape Finisterre when two galleasses that were over-masted rolled them overboard. One ship that had lost her mainmast was assisted into Donegal harbour by a turf-boat: others, like Recalde's *San Juan*, had had their mainmasts shot through and through at Calais or Gravelines so that they could "bear no weight of sail".[2] Still more had to have their masts cut down.

Rudders, too, gave trouble, especially those of the galleasses, the purely fighting type of ships. The *Gerona* was stranded with a broken rudder at Killybegs when de Leyva reached her and this had to be repaired before he could get to sea a third time for his final fatal voyage. The difficulties of the *Zuñiga* who suffered form the same disablement are recounted later.

That conditions on board the Spanish ships were fatal to health, and often to survival, is attested time and time again by the reports made to the King during the campaign, and by the statements of shipwrecked, captured prisoners examined before the English, after the battles, flight, and shipwrecks had come to an end. On the 12th/22nd a captured Portuguese sailor, who had been on board the Vice-Flagship with Admiral Recalde, admitted under examination that "four or five died every day of hunger and thirst".[3] By the time the ships fell away towards the Biscayan coast at the end of their journey that able Purser-in-Chief, Pedro Coco Calderon, reported that there was "not one drop of water" in his ship. In fact strict, severe rationing had had to be enforced,

[1] C.S.P.I., p. 93.

[2] See Ibid., pp. 39, 50, 63: C.S.P.S., pp. 292, 431, and C.S.P.V. (1581–1591), pp. 364–5.

[3] C.S.P.I., p. 39.

the Duke reported to the King, by the time that the Armada had
reached the Scottish coast earlier.

> Our provisions are so scanty that, in order to make them and
> the water last a month [by which time he hoped to have
> made Coruña], the rations of every person on the fleet, with-
> out exception, have been reduced; just enough being served
> out to keep them alive, namely, half a pound of biscuit
> [probably rotten by now], a pint of water, and half a pint of
> wine daily, without anything else. Your Majesty may
> imagine what suffering this entails in the midst of the dis-
> comfort of so long a voyage. We have consequently over
> 3,000 sick, without counting the wounded, who are
> numerous, on the fleet.[1]

The first that we learn of the Spanish ships being in distress for
want of food and water off the *Irish* coasts is prior to the 8th/18th
September when the Sovereign of Dinglecush informs Vice-
President Norreys of Munster that there are ships off the Blaskets.
The men are "sick, destitute of victual, and in great extremity".[2]
On the 9th/19th the Purser of the *Zuñiga*, Petrus Baptista,
reported under examination, that after sailing about Scotland
for Spain, the whole fleet was "in great danger for want of bread,
flesh and water".

The trouble was of long standing. Only twenty days after the
Armada had set out from Lisbon ships from almost every squadron reported that they were short of water. Casks were defective
although they had been stowed over a month before, and the
water was green and stinking. This was alarming and struck at
the lives of the crews before any encounters with the enemy had
yet taken place. Early in August, off the Flemish banks, animals
were thrown overboard,

> many of the men having died from sickness caused by bad
> and insufficient food.[3]

[1] C.S.P.S., pp. 393–4.
[2] C.S.P.I., pp. 26–7.
[3] C.S.P.S., p. 392.

Later in the same month, when the fleet was making its crazed course through one of the most treacherous races known— between Fair Isle and the Orkneys—so desperate were the men for water that they threw overboard 100 more horses and mules.[1]

As for the weather the gales of west and north-west Ireland are known to be severe and a menace to shipping, so that inhabitants of the islands and remote coastal districts often profit from salvage hauls; even to trains, one in Donegal having been blown off a viaduct in 1925. Since then anemometers to give warning of approaching gales have been installed in three of the counties that harvested disabled Spanish ships—Clare, Kerry and Donegal. Gusts of 112 miles per hour have been recorded in the first county, believed to be a record for the British Isles, and of 109 in Donegal, and those who experienced the hurricane that swept across Ireland to north-western Scotland in 1961 will not easily forget it.

Nevertheless the Dublin Meteorological Office attributes the wreck of the Spanish ships along these coasts

> to ignorance of the Irish coastline, and to bad seamanship rather than bad weather. The strongest winds ... were not strong enough to damage ships in open water. The losses were of ships caught on a lee shore, and ships sailing into headlands not on their charts.[2]

In an accompanying letter the same writer states:

> It is true that the indented coastline of the western seaboard causes considerable variations in the weather experienced. ... The difficulties of navigating there are not due to the weather, but to the complications of wind, waves, tidal currents and swell ... the regular rollers, often with a considerable distance between the crests, generated by storms as much as 1,000 miles away, that move quite independently of the local wind. It can happen that the locally-produced waves move

[1] C.S.P.I., pp. 39 and 63.
[2] *Weather in Old Dublin*, F. E. Dixon, Dub. Hist. Record, September 1959, Vol. XV.

across the swell and it is then impossible for a ship to keep headed into both at the same time.[1]

The information that local waves move *across* the swell with disastrous results for craft is of value since it helps to explain how the battered Spanish ships—some, like the Levantines, of the keelless Mediterranean type—could not keep to their course.

However, the main and most trustworthy source for prevailing conditions during September to mid-October, 1588, must always be the State Papers. In this the Director of the Meteorological Office concurs, but he confesses that "we have not consulted them directly".[2] Had he and his staff done so I believe they would reverse the opinion given above.

The most reliable accounts of the weather are given among the *Spanish State Papers*—by the Duke of Medina Sidonia in his *Diaries* to the King; by the Purser-in-Chief, Pedro Coco Calderon; by a Galician servant, Juan de Nova, by Captain Juan de Saavedra, and other surviving witnesses. For corroboration we have the reports of Captain de Cuellar and Paymaster Aramburu which will appear later in these pages. The combined reports are telling.

Take Medina Sidonia first:

> after this long-continued bad and contrary weather . . . on four separate nights heavy gales with strong winds, thick fogs and rain. . . . By God's mercy, yesterday at noon, the wind shifted to the west, somewhat more in our favour. We are therefore able to sail in a southerly direction. . . . The wind has now veered to the W.N.W. . . . Pray consider the distress of the Armada after so terrible a voyage.[3]

He wrote on August 21st, four weeks before the first Spanish ships in distress were sighted off the west of Ireland coasts. It was at this point, when the Fleet Flagship was 90 leagues north-west of Achill Head, at about 58° N, that the Duke made his final

---

[1] Letter to the author, July 7th, 1965.
[2] Letter to the author, December 24th, 1964.
[3] C.S.P.S., pp. 411–12.

muster of accompanying ships and sent off his *Sailing Orders* printed at the opening of this book. Now, if ever, was the time and place to alter course.

> Then the trouble began. For the next two weeks there were nothing but storms from the worst possible quarter, the south-west, and baffling head winds. On Saturday, September 3rd the Duke found himself, according to the pilots, still in about 58° N and perhaps farther east than he had been two weeks before. Meanwhile seventeen ships more had parted company. . . . The wind had veered for the moment to the north-east.[1]

Next, Pedro Coco Calderon:

> From the 24th [of August] to the 4th September we sailed without knowing whither, through constant storms, fogs and squalls. As this hulk could not beat to windward it was necessary to keep out at sea, and we were unable to discover the main body of the Armada until the 4th . . . when we joined it. [He then describes how he saw two ships fall away towards the Faroes and Iceland.]
>
> From the 5th–10th [of September], [having sighted some Armada ships which the heavy sea prevented them from joining] we continued to make Cape Clear [probably Erris Head], always working to windward, breaking our tackle, and taking a great deal of water. . . . On the west coast of Ireland this hulk found herself near an island . . . the sea running strongly towards the land, to the great danger of the hulk. The purser [Calderon] ordered her to tack to the north-west, which took her 30 leagues distant, and it is believed that the rest of the Armada will have done the same. If not they will certainly have lost some of the ships, as the coast is rough, the sea heavy, and the winds strong from the seaward.[2]

Coco Calderon was right in his surmise.

The reports about the galleass *Zuñiga* (one of the most fully-documented Spanish ships) who, with shattered spars and a broken

[1] Mattingly, p. 309.
[2] C.S.P.S., pp. 448–9.

rudder-pivot, like some battered bird beat back and forth in the gales for more than seven weeks, tell us even more of the savage weather. From three different sources—the reports of Captain Juan de Saavedra, in command of a company of Neapolitan soldiers on board her, from Purser Pedro de Igueldo, and from a *Relation* from Havre de Grace—we can piece together the following facts. On August 19th the *Zuñiga* passed between the Orkneys and Fair Island and on the 21st sighted "the extreme point of Ireland" (Malin or Erris Head). She then stood out to sea with other Armada ships for 15 days. On September 2nd she was in dire straits and appealed to the *San Martín* for help, but Medina Sidonia could give her none, being in evil case himself. Next, on the 7th, meeting the *San Juan* at sea with only two ships in attendance she appealed to Recalde. He too was unable to help her and gave her permission to run for Coruña as best she could. She then arrived off the coast of Ireland in foul weather "despairing of relief and in fear of running aground". Enduring variable weather for five days she found herself off "the point of Ireland" (Bray Head or Dorsey Island) "which they could not double for want of a rudder", but was driven northwards again by a south-west wind into Liscannor Creek (County Clare). Here she remained for eight days obtaining, like Recalde, supplies of food and water by force which lasted until October 4th. On September 22nd she left Liscannor with the wind astern, running before a furious gale which drove her as far south as Cape Finisterre, and then another contrary wind five days later blew her up-Channel where she made port at Havre de Grace about October 11th. "Any other ship would have been lost",[1] declares Igueldo. During the storm she threw overboard two culverins. The details of her repairs is so lengthy that one surmises she had to be practically rebuilt and one wonders that she survived at all.

Apart from the confirmation of furious gales and fickle changeable winds Saavedra's report is of interest because he reveals two facts similar to details of Aramburu's and de Cuellar's—that the *Zuñiga* took on supplies by force, the second ship known to have

[1] Ibid., pp. 458–9.

done so, the other being Recalde's; and that her Captain was originally listed as being aboard the *San Nicolas*, indicating that the absence of de Cuellar's name from the *San Pedro* in the official lists proves nothing and that there was probably a last-minute reshuffle of officers at Coruña.

Juan de Nova confirms the vile weather in the north previous to the wreck of *La Trinidad Valencera*, the Venetian merchantman, between September 14th/16th. His report interests us for another reason—because he mentions an Irishman and a Scotsman who conversed with the survivors in Latin, as the Bishop of Derry, a priest, and a third man did to Captain de Cuellar.

When we come to the *State Papers Ireland* we find the references to the weather among the examinations of the Spanish prisoners, interspersed with passing comments from the English-in-office. The shorter accounts of these men agree with the *State Papers Spanish*. The first that we hear of it causing distress to the Spanish ships is on September 8th/18th when Captains Pietro de Quibel and Pietro Rodriguez speak of three Castilian ships being driven "by stress of weather" into Dingle Bay. The doomed prisoners from these ships, examined at Tralee, tell of "contrary winds", and then of the "tempestuous weather 18 days since",[1] that is about the first of the month. And other Spaniards speak of ships being "wind-driven".

When Don Luis de Cordova was examined on October 1st/10th, he tells of how the *Falcon Blanco*, a Flemish hulk, was "driven in upon O'Flaherty's country" (Connemara). Finally James Machary of the Cross, an Irish impressed sailor, when he had been tracked down, perhaps in his native Tipperary, examined as late as December, 1588, tells how his ship (*La Duquesa Santa Ana*) was driven into Lougherris (Loughros Mor Bay, Donegal), when during the third week in September,

> there fell a great storm which brake in sunder all their cables and struck them upon ground [shipwrecked them].[2]

[1] C.S.P.I., p. 27.
[2] Ibid., pp. 98–9.

Some comments on the extraordinary weather of that autumn are given by English officials resident in Ireland, among them Edward White, Clerk of the Council of Connacht, who describes the gale of September 10th/20th as

> a most extreme wind and cruel storm, the like whereof hath not been seen or heard a long time.[1]

Writing from Castle Jordan, Sir Henry Duke whom the Lord Deputy describes as "a busybody, vain, and full of words", having sent out a spy late at night, on October 26th/November 5th, tells how the Spanish ships driven into Killybegs harbour earlier were "sore bruised by the seas", one of them "cast away without the harbour", and a second "broken to pieces on the shore".[2]

The Mayor of Waterford is informed by an Englishman in Galway that "the weather being so foul" the boats of the ships that got away to Spain could not land at Limerick: at the same time he mentions the nameless ship cast away off the baronry of Borreis. Sir Henry Wallop, Treasurer at Wars, writing from Cork city tells how the Dingle ships were turned back by the wind when they sought to get out of harbour, concluding with relief that, after their departure "there is no fear of hurt by foreign invasion this year".[3]

The Mayor of Limerick testifies that the Spaniards were "beaten by stress of weather to the coast": and the Lord Deputy, enclosing a *Brief of the Wrecks* (known up-to-date) speaks of the "tempests of September 17/18th and 27th/28th with the probable loss of the Admiral (Recalde) in them."[4] (In this, of course he was wrong.) Even Byngham, not given to exaggeration, says that after the great ship (*La Duquesa Santa Ana*) left Ballicro the weather became "very stormy and foul", and he asks pardon for not sending prisoners more hastily owing to "the great floods" which were impassable.[5]

---

[1] C.S.P.I., Vol. 136, p. 57.
[2] Ibid., p. 64.
[3] & [4] Ibid., pp. 39 and 41.
[5] Ibid., pp. 48-9.

Many more calendared references to the wild weather of the autumn of 1588 might be added. Among writers of this century, Spotswood-Green who knew the Irish coasts intimately, sums up the prevailing temper of that season most clearly of all:

During the whole time that the Armada was beating her terrible retreat the wind was more oftener southerly than in any other point. It varied chiefly from south to south-west, and in spite of this some of the ships made their way to wind-ward, or at least were able to maintain a southerly course, which proves, I think, that they were able to sail successfully within about six points of the wind. Others probably had no weatherly qualities at all, only made way when they got the wind abaft the beam, and had to run before every gale.

The weather all over the British area was exceptionally stormy: cyclone followed cyclone, those of August 23–24, September 2nd and 10th [O.S.] being the heaviest. It was in this last north-westerly gale that most of the wrecks occurred. . . . Cyclonic conditions prevailed until after October. [1]

Finally, faulty maps causing blind ignorance of the Irish coasts were a grave and often fatal source of danger to the Spanish fleet. For the maps depicting the west coast of Ireland were so insanely out of scale they failed to indicate that the north coast of Mayo juts out forty miles westward into the sea; or to depict the precipitous cliffs without creeks, excluding all possibility of shelter for craft either large or small. Thus dissensions amongst the commanding officers; the ships' faulty construction; the starvation, illness and death of the crews; the savage-wild weather; and incorrect maps, all combined to work against the weakened battle-and-weather-beaten fleet.

[1] Ibid, pp. 447–8.

3

Arrival of the Ships on the Irish Coasts: Dates of the Wrecks

DURING September the prevailing winds continued to force those ships which had parted company with the *San Martín* relentlessly inshore. Meanwhile the intense damp and cold, which those born in Mediterranean countries were unfit to resist, took its toll of the men already suffering from typhus, thirst and starvation. Many of the ships riddled with cannon shot had leaks which could not be kept under, necessitating constant pumping. The wonder is, not that so many foundered, but that so large a number got home to Spain.

In the first week of the month the ships were spied coasting along, seeking harbourage, most of their captains and pilots ignorant of where they were, "in great extremity for want of knowledge", according to a Scotsman seized by Medina Sidonia at sea, who reported to the "Suffrein of Dinglecush".[1] We must picture the ships dropping down on the west coast of Ireland from the north-west. "Those most to windward would reach Kerry, others Clare, Galway and Mayo; while the leeward ships, failing to weather the north-west corner of Mayo [Erris Head] would fall away into Donegal Bay." More or less in this order the ships arrived, but some "tacking to the north-west gained an offing before the wind veered, and so escaped",[2] including Coco Calderon's *San Salvador*.

The emotions of the Spaniards bearing down on the Irish coasts were confused. Various survivors indicate that if they escaped shipwreck they looked for "friendship and good treat-

[1] C.S.P.I., p. 27.
[2] Spotswood-Green, p. 436.

ment" at the hands of a people who had kept their common
Faith, in spite of persecution and decimation by organized famine
and military slaughter. But the Spaniards, especially those soldiers
seasoned in battle, or the mariners who had sailed with Admiral
Juan Martinez de Recalde, were a realistic people, given to irony,
and accustomed to face danger with immense courage and a faith
which transcended visions of death, torture, imprisonment, starvation and exile. This is obvious in the accounts of both Aramburu
and Captain de Cuellar. If they did not receive succour and
shelter on land this would be the will of God and He, together
with Our Lady and the company of Heaven, would care for
them.

The minds and emotions of the English in command of the
mixed forces on shore were equally confused. As the great ships,
larger than any that had ever been seen by either English or Irish,
were sighted drifting off the coasts, stranded on shoals, or wrecked
on reefs and invisible rocks that pierced their hulls, the Governors
of provinces, the Clerks to the Council, the sheriffs, mayors, the
Attorney General and Lord Chief Justice and others sent off their
despatches to Lord Deputy Fitzwylliam in Dublin, or to the Privy
Council in England; to Burghley, Walsyngham and others at
home, with the utmost speed possible in those days when fleetness
of foot, mount, or sail counted more than brute strength or
superb intelligence.

The doubts that assailed the English in Ireland were many.
Would the Irish princes and chiefs of septs, who had given human
pledges, and their word to be faithful to the English, remain so?
The bands of trained men were small. Those in charge of them
were not only unprepared for such an eventuality as the arrival
of the "strange ships" but uncertain of their ability to handle this
unprecedented event. Had they enough men to capture and
restrain as many as double, sometimes treble, the number of their
own armed men? Would the Irish who had come over to them
stand firm in their new duties, or revert to their former ways of
looting and hiding treasure, of sheltering the enemy? Would the
Irish in a body rise up and ally themselves with the Spaniards if

the latter arrived in large numbers, and "Her Majesty be dis-possessed of Ireland" as the Lord Deputy himself put it?[1] Whence came the ships, direct from Spain—a new Armada, in fact—or from England? In what condition were the ships and men?

Writing to the Lord Deputy on September 8th/18th from Athlone, Sir Richard Byngham, Governor of Connacht, discloses some of these fears:

> Even [just] now I received the enclosed letter . . . by which your Lordship shall perceive some further news of strange ships: whether they be of the dispersed fleet which are fled from the supposed overthrow in the Narrow Seas [the English Channel], or new forces come from Spain directly, no man is able to advertise otherwise, than by guess, which doth rather show their coming from Spain, both by these falling from the west, and the others which coasted along the north parts of Sligo, but I expect very present news either from one place or the other, for by all likelihoods they mind to land. I look this night for my horses to be here, and upon receipt of further intelligence I will make towards the sea coast, either upwards to Thomond or downwards to Sligo. The board which was found in the cock-boat I send herewith to your Lordship, in which is some mystery hidden under the 'burne' of three letters; but it should seem to be a mark under the K.P., the Catholic King's name.[2]

Byngham then petitions for

> lasts of powder with lead and match in the store here, for it is the thing we shall greatly want if stirs arise. . . . Also I think it were very convenient to levy a band of footmen of this country people . . . such as have been soldiers, for if service come on we shall lack them, and prevent their going away to the enemy, which is like enough else they will . . . [being] idle men . . .

The brothers Hovenden, Richard and Henry, under-agents of the great Hugh O'Neill, Earl of Tyrone, in the north were also in doubt:

[1] & [2] C.S.P.I., pp. 98 and 29.

We are 150 men and will, God willing, be doing with the Spaniards as we may find our best advantage, though we are in doubt whether the country will be true to us or not.[1]

"There were 6 or 7 hundred men at least landed" [from *La Gerona*]. "1,500 sails of Spaniards were rumoured to be setting forth to land".! A spy sent out to report had been taken up by O'Dogherty's, the Lord of Inishowen's men, so that they had "no certain news". One senses the urgency and uncertainty in the writers' hearts.

The first ships sighted from land were seen on September 5th/15th and reported by George Byngham, sheriff of Sligo and brother of the Governor of Connacht, writing from the strong castle of Ballymote. "Three Spanish ships which bore down towards the harbour of Calebeg",[2] that is Killybegs in Donegal, a favourite trading harbour of the Spaniards, well-known to their merchants. On the same day the sheriff of Clare, Boethius Clanshee (M'Glannough) who had gone over to the English, reported "seven ships from Flanders and Spain arrived before Caryge-e-colle", that is Carigaholt twenty miles from Limerick, at the mouth of the Shannon. The man who reported them was the coroner (the officer charged with maintaining the property of the Crown) of Clare, and he "parleyed with the Spaniards",[3] the first to do so it would seem. One wonders what tongue they spoke in, pidgin-English, Gaelic, or a universal sign-language, and how they appeared to the Irish and English. For these were not shipwrecked men. Presumably they came ashore in cock-boats or other small craft to reconnoitre, which they must have done successfully. For not only did six of the seven ships get away on a favourable wind to Spain, on the 12th/22nd—the seventh ship, the *San Marcos* was so badly damaged she had to be burnt—but not a man of them appears either to have been taken prisoner or to have been killed. The arrival of the Shannon ships caused more excitement than that of any of the others, with the exception of

1 & 2 C.S.P.I., pp. 35–6 and 28.
3 C.S.P.I., pp. 29–30.

those in Blasket Sound, perhaps because the good pilotage of the Spaniards earned them admiration, or merely because they were the first reported, apart from the Killybegs ships, whose men did not land so swiftly.

From then onwards reports of ships riding at anchor, coasting along the shores, stranded or wrecked off the northern or western coasts of Ireland came in like flocks of starlings—ships near the Aran Islands, "more seen westward from the islands",[1] Clare Island, Clew Bay, Tralee, Dinglecush and the Blaskets; in "O'Dogherty's country", that is Inishowen, the promontory in the north then called an island; in ne Sweeny ne Doe's, west of Lough Swilly; in O'Flaherty's in Connemara; beneath Turlough O'Brien's tower off the dark Cliffs of Moher, at unpronounceable, unintelligible places to English ears like Burrishoole and Ballycrowhie: reports of men drowned, starving, killed or escaped, men wearing chains of gold about their necks, or velvet capes embroidered with gold upon their shoulders.

Scarcely a ship is named in the *State Papers Ireland*. The men on shore could not see their names and, unless an interpreter were present, could not glean from survivors the outlandish names even when they were given by the Spaniards. The contrast between Protestant England, as she had then in large part become, and Catholic Spain is epitomized by the ships' names in the two fleets, the English bearing such simple, clipt ones as the *Black Crow*, the *Bear*, the *Bull*, *Cygnet* and *Dolphin*, the *Tiger*, *Lion*, *Antelope*, *Swallow* and *Little Swan*; ships with feminine names, perhaps in remembrance of the Captain's or owner's wife or sweetheart— the *Elizabeth Jonas* or *Mary Rose*; after men, whether royal, saintly, or legendary—the *Charles*, the *George*, the *Edward Bonaventure*, the *Philip-Mary* and *Merlin*; ships with abstract fanciful names—the *Hope*, *Nonpareil*, *Fantasy*, *Foresight*, *Revenge*, *Swiftsure* and *Triumph*; names to do with the earth and the sky—the *Primrose*, *Rainbow*, *Sun* and *Moon*; names classical, of which the English Navy has always been fond, like the *Achates*. But when we come to the Armada ships, with hardly an exception they

[1] C.S.P.I., pp. 29–30.

carry religious names, being dedicated to a Saint, to Our Lady, to Feasts of the Church, to the *Holy Spirit* and the *Crucifixion*: to male Saints like Peter, Matthew, John, Nicholas, Gabriel, Anthony, Bernard and Bartholomew: and among the female, Anne, Barbara and Magdalen. Our Lady is commemorated frequently by her *Conception*, *Assumption* and *Coronation*, by her *Rosary* or *Chaplet of Flowers*, and by her powers of *Succour*. Only when we come to the galleys, rowed by slaves, do we find more ordinary names—*Captain*, *Princess* and *Diana*. The English, when faced with the Spanish religious ships'-names, merely cut them short. In the same way that *costoletta d'agnello* becomes *chop*, or *inchiostro ink*, the great Italian merchantman *La Sancta Maria Rata Encoronada* became the *Rat*!

It was estimated by one writer, the Attorney General, Sir John Popham, writing to Burghley on September 10th/20th from Cork, that as many as 59 ships all told had been sighted, and the consensus of opinion was that 16–17 had perished, a number still held to by many modern writers. The ships' sizes had also to be gauged by guess-work, the same writer declaring that two of the seven ships in the Shannon were

taken to be of a thousand tons apiece, two more of 400 tons the piece, and three small barks [sic][1].

The havoc wrought by shipwreck on the coasts of Ireland in 1588 took place in just six weeks to the day. An exhaustive examination of the *State Papers Ireland*, and *Spanish*, discloses that the ships about to be wrecked began to be reported on September 5th/15th. The first one wrecked whose name we know was *La Trinidad Valencera* on September 14th/16th, and the last *La Gerona* on October 26th. Out of the twenty-five ships postulated by Spotswood-Green thirteen are unnamed and only twelve named. Few ships were given names by the English until the examinations of prisoners had revealed them, or they were learnt from the jumbled reports which survivors made when recounting their adventures to one another long afterwards, sometimes confusing

[1] C.S.P.I., p. 31.

the ships' names, thus making another tangle to unravel. For example *Nuestra Señora de la Rosario* was invariably confused with *Nuestra Señora de la Rosa*, ships of different squadrons and types, and the three ships in which Don Alonso de Leyva was wrecked caused further confusion. Sometimes we have to wait until a ship's officer sends in his report, or search some allusive reference in an ambassador's letters, or Medina Sidonia's *Diary*, to find confirmation of a suspected truth concerning a single ship.

Taking the twelve named ships we can make the following chronological table:

DATES OF THE ARMADA NAMED SHIPS WRECKED, STRANDED, OR BURNT OFF THE COASTS OF IRELAND
September–October, 1588
(in chronological order)

SHIP	TYPE	TON- NAGE	SQUADRON	OFFICER IN COMMAND OF SQUADRON, or other person of note associated with her	SITE OF WRECK	DATE (New Style)
La Trinidad Valencera	Large Merchant- man (Venetian)	1,100	Levantine	Martin de Bertondona	Glenagiv- ney Bay, Donegal	14–16 Sept.
S.M. or *N.S. de la Rosa*	Large Merchant- man	945	Vice- Flagship, Guipuz- coan	Miguel de Oquendo (Capt. (?) Martin de Villa Franca)	Blasket Sound, Kerry	21 Sept.
San Marcos	Galleon	790	"Of Portugal"	Admiral Juan Mar- tinez de Recalde	Scattery Roads, Shannon	,,
La Sancta Maria Rata Encoronada	Large Merchant- man	820	Levantine	Martin de Bertondona (Don Alonso de Leyva)	Blacksod Bay, Mayo	,,

SHIP	TYPE	TON-NAGE	SQUADRON	OFFICER IN COMMAND OF SQUADRON, or other person of note associated with her	SITE OF WRECK	DATE (New Style)
El Grangrin	Large Merchant-man	1,160	Vice Flagship, Biscayan	Adm. Juan Martinez de Recalde (Don Pedro de Mendoza)	Clare Island, Mayo	21–22 Sept.
San Juan* (of Ragusa)	?	?	Levantine (?)	Captain (?) Fernando Horra	Blasket Sound, Kerry	22 or 23 Sept.
La Lavia or Labia†	Large Merchant-man	728	Vice Flagship, Levantine	Martin de Bertondona (Aranda and de Cuellar)	Streedagh Strand, Sligo	24–25 Sept.
San Juan	Galleon	530	Castilian	Adm. Diego Flores de Valdés (Don Diego Enriquez)	,,	,,
A third unnamed ship	?	?	?	?	,,	,,
La Duquesa Santa Ana	Hulk	900	Andalu-sian	Don Pedro de Valdés (Don Alonso de Leyva)	Loughros Mor Bay, Donegal	25–26 Sept.
Falcon Blanco	Flemish Hulk, "mediano"	300	Hulks	Juan Gomez de Medina (Don Luis de Cordova)	Off Davillaun Isle, Connemara	,,
La Juliana	Large Merchant-man	860	Levantine	Martin de Bertondona	Gola Isle, Donegal	Sept. ?

SHIP	TYPE	TON-NAGE	SQUADRON	OFFICER IN COMMAND OF SQUADRON, or other person of note associated with her	SITE OF WRECK	DATE (New Style)
La Gerona, or Girona	Galleass	Not given	"Of Naples"	Don Hugo de Moncada (Don Alonso de Leyva)	Bush Foot. W. of the Giant's Causeway	28 Oct.

* There is a mystery about this ship, which may have been one of the *San Juan Bautistas*, but whose name is given by Aramburu merely as *San Juan*. Ragusa, the old port of Dubrovnik, was one of the greatest of the Mediterranean ports, rivalling Venice. One would choose this Ragusa rather than the inland town of the same name in Sicily. But there is no *San Juan* among the Levantine ships listed except "de Sicilia". This ship is stated by Laughton to have gone down in the North Sea, but it is possible that Horra's *San Juan* is in fact the disabled *de Sicilia* after all.

† Spotswood-Green suggests that it is on this ship that the Judge Advocate and Captain de Cuellar foundered, but he gives no proof for this statement; nor does de Cuellar give her name, merely stating that she was from the Levant.

The basis of this table is from the *Full Statement of the Armada sailing from Lisbon* (C.S.P.S., pp. 280-3) sent to the King by the Duke of Medina Sidonia, 9 May 1588. The dates are chiefly derived from a careful scrutiny of the C.S.P. Ireland.

The problems posed by the arrival of large numbers of Spaniards alive—sometimes they took two or three days to land treasure and provisions from a ship before fortifying themselves in old forts or castles—were considerable and baffling to the English or the English-affected Irish in remote districts. Large numbers of Spaniards were killed out of fear, because their captors had not enough men or buildings to restrain them, for lack of immediate direction from those above them in power—the Lord Deputy or Governors of provinces—or from a desire to earn merit and reward, whether land, castles or financial remuneration. The slaughter made by a single Irish Goliath—Melaghlin M'Cabb who "killed 80 Spaniards with his galloglas axe"[1] is fearful to imagine. An able, hardened soldier like Sir George Carew, who

[1] C.S.P.I., p. 40.

was to be in at the death of Gaelic Ireland with his successes at Kinsale and Dunboy, informed Walsyngham on the 18th/28th, from Dublin, that he estimated roundly that

> 3,000 Spaniards who came to land by swimming etc., [were] slain, besides about 2,000 drowned between Loughfoyle and the Dingle.[1]

This omits the wrecks south of the Dingle, on the coast of Clare, and possibly that of *La Gerona* east of Lough Foyle. The next day Secretary Fenton was writing to Burghley from Dublin that they had

> ... no certain knowledge before yesterday of the quality or number of the Spaniards.[2]

He encloses an estimate of a higher figure than Carew's—"5,394 drowned, killed and taken upon the coast of Ireland". Carew in a second note, this time to Burghley, shrewdly admits a

> doubtfulness of the Irish before the victory was known to be Her Majesty's.[3]

The result of all this uncertainty was appeals to England for men, munitions and money, from the Lord Deputy and Council, and the Governors of Provinces to Lord Burghley and the Privy Council. Five days after the arrival of the first Spanish ships the Lord Deputy in Dublin Castle roundly stated:

> We have neither men, money nor munition to answer these extraordinary services.[4]

Two days later, on September 12th/22nd he wrote in cold blood:

> There are not 750 foot in bands in the whole realm. [We] cannot impress the few soldiers for the shoeing of their horses. We look rather to be overrun by the Spaniards than otherwise.[5]

[1] & [2] C.S.P.I., pp. 40 and 43.
[3], [4] & [5] C.S.P.I., pp. 42, 30 and 35.

On 14th/24th the hated Byngham, who feared the union of Spaniards harboured with O'Rourke, and of O'Rourke with the powerful northern chieftains, asked for footbands.

Informed of the situation and of these appeals from Ireland the Queen acted with alacrity. On 14th/24th she issued an order.

Queen Elizabeth to Sir Richard Greenville [sic]
   Where we have some occasion offered to us by reason of certain ships of the Spanish Armada that came about Scotland and are driven to sundry parts in the West of Ireland, to put in readiness some forces to be sent into Ireland, as further occasion shall be given us, which we mean to be shipped in the river of Severn, to pass from thence to Waterford or Cork, we have thought meet to make choice of you for this service following.
[Drake was occupied elsewhere.]
   We require you that upon the north coasts of Devon and Cornwall, towards Severn, you make stay of all shipping meet to transport soldiers to Waterford, and to give charge that the same ships be made ready with masters, mariners, and all other maritime provisions needful, so as upon the next warning given from us or from our Council they may be ready to receive our said soldiers, which shall be 300 out of Cornwall and Devon, and 400 out of Gloucestershire and Somersetshire. We have also some other further intention to use your service in Ireland with these ships aforesaid, whereof Sir Walter Rawley [sic], knight, whom we have acquainted withal shall inform you, who also hath a disposition for our service to pass into Ireland, either with these forces or before that they shall depart.[1]

The times were grave. On the following day she issued orders *To the Lieutenants of Counties* "for putting men in readiness to march for Ireland within an hour's warning".[2] On the third day, the 16th/26th, the Lord Deputy put in a plea to Walsyngham

to hasten five or six ships from Bristol to the Irish coast to destroy the 40 sea-beaten vessels returning into Spain.[3]

1 & 2 & 3 C.S.P.I., pp. 37–8–9.

But by September 18th/28th, with the departure and wreck of
more Spanish ships in the west, Fitzwylliam is calmer and writes:

> The soldiers coming from England may be stayed. We had
> not 10 pounds in money to imprest for this mighty service.[1]

But Byngham appealed for further forces against O'Rourke and
his harboured Spaniards.

In October trouble began to flare up afresh in the north. The
Spaniards come ashore from the two great ships wrecked in
Inishowen and eastward near Dunluce Castle, the influx of
Scottish from the Isles come to aid their Irish brethren, and the
uncertainty of whether the Irish and Scottish in conjunction with
the Spaniards might not rise in force against England, once again
alarmed those in authority in Ireland. Men from Cheshire and
Lancashire, counties nearer to the northern coasts of Ireland—
200 men for whom the Mayor of Liverpool was to provide
shipping—were ordered by the Privy Council sitting at St. James's
Palace to be levied by the Earl of Derby. On the last day of the
month the Earl of Pembroke was commanded to levy troops to
repair to the castles of Beaumaris and Chester, the Privy Council
alleging that

> 1,500 Spaniards whose ships have been cast away on the north
> of Ireland, have combined with the Irish.[2]

As late as October 29th/November 8th the Privy Council in
England informed the Lord Deputy in Ireland that they were
sending over 2,000 men under the former Lord Deputy, Sir John
Perrott, better-loved by the Irish. Another further 500 were to
be drawn from the Irish chiefs in the north favourable to England.
Then comes a trenchant piece of advice:

> And because we perceive by your Lordship's said letters that
> the Spaniards are in such numbers, with the assistance of the
> Irishry, as you cannot well make head against them, we have
> thought good to advise your Lordship not to hazard the fight

[1] C.S.P.I., p. 41.
[2] Ibid., p. 70.

with them, except it be upon special and apparent advantage, until these supplies [of men] may come unto you.[1]

In other words, Fitzwylliam was to employ delaying tactics, similar to the brilliant ones employed by O'Neill, who in his youth in England and Wales had learnt diplomacy in the castles and great houses of Sir Henry Sydney and the Earl of Leicester. Such advice would hardly be acceptable to a man of action, a soldier like Fitzwylliam, who had ten days earlier told the Council to "stay the men" formerly requested, and who had written to Walsyngham the day before the Privy Council wrote to him assuring them that:

> Since it hath pleased God by His hand upon the rocks to drown the greater and better sort of them [the shipwrecked Spaniards] I will, with His favour, be His soldier for the despatching of those ragges which yet remain.[2]

But in London, as well as on the continent and in parts of Ireland, false rumours were rampant. It was said that Medina Sidonia had been wrecked with the *San Martín*—Santa Cruz's Fleet Flagship which he had been placed aboard without any sense of glory: that he had been captured, or received along with Don Alonso de Leyva and 600 men "from land" into *La Duquesa Santa Ana* and had then been "cast away", that is lost, at sea. *Advices from London* reported that the body of Admiral Recalde "had been found drowned", together with that of the young Prince d'Ascoli, in Blasket Sound.

No one knew for certain what was happening in "the dark continent" of Ireland except those on the spot—and as we have seen even they could be confused. The tireless Lord Deputy, growing old and worn with long service, had yet to make his winter's journey into the north and west. Sir Richard Byngham, avaricious like all the other Englishmen who had risked their lives in putting down both shipwrecked Spaniards and Irish "savages", made a bid for a lease of the long-naved Cistercian

---

[1] C.S.P.I., p. 69, from a draft corrected by Burghley, from Dublin Castle.
[2] Ibid., p. 68.

Abbey of Boyle and its fertile lands "in consideration of his great charges in opposing the Spaniards".[1]

Earlier in the summer it had been said that Drake—always a magnet to draw the Spaniards' eyes since they feared his quick-silver-way of appearing and disappearing, generally after he had sacked, burnt and plundered—was wounded, captured or killed. Now it was stated that he had lost a leg. The news was furnished by an Irish student from the cathedral city of Armagh who had accidentally been swept up into the English fleet, from which he escaped. He declared that it was current knowledge among the English, and that the misfortune had occurred "during the fighting with the flagship of the Armada". Again, Drake was going to the Indies or, a much more likely rumour, he was putting to sea "with a squadron of ships . . . in search of stragglers from the Armada".[2]

[1] C.S.P.I., p. 77.
[2] C.S.P.S., pp. 413, 450–1, 474.

4

Captain de Cuellar's Narrative Letter and its Significance

AMONG survivors of the Spanish Armada Captain Françisco de Cuellar holds a unique position since he alone has left an account of his shipwreck, off the west coast of Ireland in September, 1588, and his adventures thereafter covering more than a year as a fugitive in Ireland and a refugee in Scotland. The narrative was first published by a Spanish naval officer, Captain Cesareo Fernández Duro, in his *La Armada Invencible* (1884–5), in which he drew on unpublished material in the great Archives of Simancas and the Academy of History at Madrid. A solitary writer in the British Isles, the Earl of Ducie, commented on it in the following year. In 1891 the historian Froude published three articles on the Spanish Armada, including passages from de Cuellar, which excited further interest. But it was not until 1893 that de Cuellar's account was translated into English, by Professor O'Reilly, and subsequently by two other writers, H. D. Sedgwick, and Robert Crawford for Hugh Allingham.[1] Although the narrative is familiar to those conversant with the historical period, and to the Irish more than to the English because of its setting, it is still not so well known as it deserves to be: nor to my knowledge has it been edited fully with notes, and descriptions of the places mentioned. Furthermore, since its translation, fresh studies on the Armada and the sixteenth century in general have been made, throwing new light on this Spanish survivor's problems and the historical background.

So far we have only one other published contemporary Armada account relevant to Ireland: and this is of ships' adven-

---

[1] Sedgwick, New York, 1895, and Allingham/Crawford, London, 1897.

tures off the west coast, a kind of log kept by Controller and Paymaster Marcos de Aramburu of the Galleons of Castile, the squadron to which de Cuellar's *San Pedro* was attached. But Aramburu never went on land so that his account is in no way comparable to the Captain's. This was not translated into English until 1909: parts of it are included herein.

Françisco de Cuellar's narrative is unique, and valuable because of its revelations about conditions in Ireland, and the Irish in those still Gaelic days before the customs of their fathers had been sedulously extinguished by English government officials and colonists. An eye-witness and participant, the Spanish Captain could view everything with a detached unbiased mind since he was neither English nor Irish, nor attached to the military forces of either country. This gives a freshness and vitality to his style. His observations are made with intelligence and recorded with clarity. His descriptions of contemporary Irish life, customs, appearance and manners of the people are vivid and unconscious, since he was writing to a personal friend, and not for court perusal or publication.

We know almost nothing about the man, the writer. He himself tells us that he was "in command of a galleon", and later that "he sailed in the *San Pedro*". This ship is listed in the *Full Statement of the Armada sailing from Lisbon sent to the King by the Duke of Medina Sidonia*, on May 19th, 1588,[1] as being under the command of Diego Flores de Valdés, where she is given as being of 530 tons, having 24 guns and a complement of 272 men, 141 of them soldiers and 131 sailors. In the Duke's *Coruña Muster held on the Royal Armada* on July 13th the number of soldiers on this ship has been increased to 184, and that of the sailors decreased to 90, making a total of 274.[2] In these lists the names of those in command of individual ships do not appear and there is therefore no mention of de Cuellar. Were it not for the kindness of the Director of the *Archivo General de Simancas* we should have little corroboration of de Cuellar's own statement, since Duro's lists

[1] C.S.P.S., pp. 280–3.
[2] Ibid., pp. 339–43.

add nothing to what we find in the published *State Papers*. Upon application to the Director he courteously made a search among the many bundles of indexed, but as yet unanalysed, papers for 1588-9. He informs me that he found that 'bundle 221 of the *Military and Naval Section*' yields the following facts:

> In a printed account by Pedro Paz Salas, in which he enumerates all the ships making up the expedition and their crews, the galleon *San Pedro*, 530 tons, had on board 131 sailors and 141 fighting men; her Captain was Don Pedro de Mendoza who had 111 men under him, and with him went Don Diego Maldonado, in command of 30 soldiers. In the same account there are listed among the *entretenidos*—that is the aspirants to posts receiving pay while waiting—a certain Captain Françisco de Cuellar, who was paid 25 *escudos* and was accompanied by his servant; also by a certain Diego de Cuellar, whose salary was 10 *escudos*.[1]

It appears from other references in the *State Papers* that officers were sometimes transferred from one ship to another after the official lists were drawn up, or between the Armada's adventures on setting out from Lisbon and reaching Coruña, and this is evidently what happened in the case of de Cuellar, for it will be seen from the extract from the letter given above that he is not as yet stated to be in charge of the *San Pedro*.

His career was to be a stormy one in more senses than one. He was not in command of the galleon for long. Having been saved from hanging at the yard-arm for some groundless, suspected misdemeanour, he was transferred to the unidentified ship, possibly *La Lavia*, or *Labia*, of the fleet's Judge Advocate, Martin de Aranda. In this ship he remained from August 10th or 11th until she was wrecked off Ireland in September.

The Simancas biographies and dictionaries, also kindly examined by the Director, yield no other facts about de Cuellar than those given in the unwieldy bundles. But his surname, and a prayer which he made to *Our Lady of Ontañar* at that moment

---

[1] Letter to the author, March 16th, 1965.

when he was poised between life and death, give us an inkling of his place of birth. Now *de* Cuellar signifies that he or his forbears came from the town of that name in Segovia, north of Madrid. The Roman city, capital of the province, lay for a thousand years like some rocky seabed beneath the ebb and flow of fluctuatng Moorish and Christian influences. For long Segovia was popu- lated by mountaineers from the north, turbulent people accus- tomed to breed cattle for their living (like the Irish who sheltered de Cuellar), and to fighting for survival. It was a city of what we in England have called the *marches*, the borderlands lying be- tween different types of country and differing races, disputable fought-over land, remaining first in the hands of one race and then of the other. In Spanish this march is known as the *entre- madura*, "the region to the south of the Douro with its apex at the junction of the sierras of Avila and the Guadarrama". Its inhabitants have been described as being

> robust and reckless, so hardy that they despised the heats of summer, could bear any excess in wine, and had no fear of death.[1]

Recall these characteristics when reading de Cuellar's experiences, what he, although not a man given to exaggeration or self-pity, himself calls "his great misfortunes".

About forty miles from the town of Cuellar there is a famous shrine dedicated to Our Lady of Hontañares, as it is called today. At the spot where she is believed to have appeared there are a number of springs, and a fountain and shrine of the seventeenth century. In de Cuellar's time it was called the *Shrine of Our Lady of Ontañar*. Its site is one of the most beautiful in the surrounding sierra. In September, the month in which de Cuellar made his desperate supplication, a great annual pilgrimage took, and still takes place to it, composed of crowds from the neighbouring villages as well as from Riaza. Now a man in what the Spaniards call "the moment of truth" only prays to a protector close to his heart, "closer than hands or feet", with whom he has been

---

[1] Havelock Ellis, *The Soul of Spain*, Constable, 1937, pp. 328 et seq.

familiar all his life, to whom he has probably committed himself from his earliest years onward, and in whom he has overpowering faith. This supplication of de Cuellar's in what he thought was the hour of his death would therefore seem to be linked with his birth or boyhood. Probably it was his mother who taught him a devotion to "Our Lady of the Springs" close to his home. He implies that his survival is due to this prayer since, as he himself describes, his surrounding companions at sea—the good Judge Advocate to whom he owed his life, the endearing Diego Enriquez and others—were all drowned before his eyes in highly distressing circumstances.

Before committing the reader to Captain de Cuellar's narrative it is well to point out something which historians have ignored— the native taboo against rescuing the drowning. The Irish have been criticized (in the *State Papers* and elsewhere) for not succouring those expiring in the water. Apart from the fact that most of the native people could not swim there was also the strong reluctance to interfere not only with a man's destiny or fate, but with the sea-god, Lir's, ancient rights. An Anglo-Irishman who knew the Irish country-people well has written:

> Along this coast [Connemara—where some of the Spanish ships were wrecked] it is considered most unlucky to save a man from drowning. 'The sea must have its due'. If you save a man, you or one of your family will most certainly be taken instead. The same belief is held in the Orkney and Shetland Islands [where two other Spanish ships foundered] and there are many people on the east coast of Scotland who will not even lift a dead body from the sea into a boat. 'It belongs to the sea'. Among some of the tribes of central and south-east Africa there is a similar reluctance to help a drowning man. To do so will bring misfortune on the rescuer. Closely connected with this idea was the custom among the Vikings of Scandinavia, as it was also among many primitive people, to fasten one or more human beings to the rollers over which a ship or war-canoe was launched.[1]

[1] Robert Gibbings, *Lovely is the Lee*, London, 1945, pp. 22 et seq.

Sir Walter Scott uses this primitive belief in his novel *The Pirate*, set in the Shetland Isles. These superstitions, older than Christianity and formerly universal, are extant in parts of England and Wales today. It is only fair to the Irish folk of 1588 to exonerate them from charges of cruelty and indifference; and in the case of one wreck in the north we have written proof among the *Spanish State Papers* of the men rowing out to, and helping survivors.

Now let de Cuellar speak for himself.

NARRATIVE *LETTER* OF CAPTAIN FRANÇISCO DE CUELLAR*

LETTER FROM ONE WHO WENT WITH THE ARMADA TO ENGLAND, GIVING HIS ACCOUNT OF THE EXPEDITION†

I believe you will be amazed to see this letter,(1) for you can have had but little confidence in my being alive. It is to assure you of this fact that I am now writing, and at some length, as I have been given cause enough by the very great tribulations and misfortunes I have suffered since the day the Armada left Lisbon for England, from all of which our Lord in His infinite mercy delivered me. I have had no opportunity to write to you for over a year, nor could I do so before God brought me to these States of Flanders, whither I came twelve days ago with all those Spaniards who had escaped from the ships wrecked in Ireland, Scotland and Shetland, being more than twenty of the largest in the Armada. In them came a great army of splendid infantrymen, many captains, ensigns, camp-masters and other officers of war, as well as many gentlemen and scions of the nobility; yet out of all these [the latter] numbering more than two hundred, not five escaped,(2) and all the rest died by drowning, or having succeeded in swimming ashore were hacked to pieces by the English

---

* Newly translated out of the Spanish by Frances Partridge.

† Probably added when the documents where first catalogued. First published in Duro's *La Armada Invencible*, Madrid, 1885.

Interleaved notes beginning on page 45 (Author).

garrisons maintained by the Queen in the kingdom of Ireland.(3)

Having most earnestly commended my soul to our Lord and the Most Holy Virgin His Mother, I was delivered from the sea and my enemies, in company with more than three hundred soldiers who had managed to save themselves and swim to land. With them I endured great hardships, living for more than seven months of that winter naked and barefoot in the mountains and forests, among the savages (4) that inhabit those regions of Ireland where we were wrecked.

It does not seem right to me that I should fail to describe, nor for you to be left in ignorance of the unjust and grievous wrongs with which I was threatened, although I had in no way failed of my duty, from which our Lord delivered me. Having been condemned to an ignominious death, as you will doubtless have heard, and seeing the inflexibility with which the order for execution was given, I demanded with much energy and anger why they were treating me so shamefully and outrageously when I had served the King as a good soldier (5) and a loyal subject in my encounters with the enemy's fleet, in all of which the galleon I commanded (6) had been very badly damaged, with many dead and wounded. And I desired them to give me a copy of the order, and that evidence should be taken from the three hundred and fifty men on board the galleon, saying that if any one of them considered me to blame they might cut me in pieces.

They refused to listen to me or to the many gentlemen who interceded on my behalf, saying that the Duke had retired to his cabin in a melancholy mood and did not wish anyone to speak with him; for besides the disastrous outcome of his meetings with the enemy, he had on the very day of my misfortune heard that two of the Portuguese galleons, the San Mateo and the San Felipe,(7) with two camp-masters on board, Don Françisco de Toledo (brother of the Conde de Orgaz) (8) and Don Diego Pimentel (brother of the Marqués de Távara), had been lost at sea and that nearly all those they carried had been cut to pieces and killed. As a result of this news the Duke shut himself in his stateroom, and his councillors made up for his stubbornness by

committing outrages right and left on the lives and reputations of
men who were guiltless, as is well-known to everyone.

The galleon San Pedro, *in which I sailed, had received much*
damage in many places from the enemy's heaviest cannon balls,
and although this was speedily remedied as well as could be done
there were still several hidden shot-holes which let in a great
deal of water. After the fierce battle fought off Calais from early
morning until seven o'clock in the evening of the 8th of August,
which was the last battle of all, our Armada began to withdraw
as I am loth to tell, and the enemy fleet followed close behind to
drive us away from their shores. When this had been safely
accomplished, which was on the 10th day of the same month,
and the enemy were seen to have fallen behind, (9) some of the
ships of the Armada began to repair their damage. On that same
day I was resting a little for my sins, for I had not slept at all for
ten days nor stopped to attend to my needs, when one of my
navigators, a worthless fellow, got under sail without saying a
word to me, and went some miles ahead of the flag-ship, as some
of the other ships had done to repair their damage. When he was
about to lower sail and see where the galleon was shipping
water, a pinnace came alongside of us, with a summons from the
Duke for me to go to the flag-ship. I went thither, but before I
reached her, orders had been given on another ship that I and
another gentleman called Don Cristóbal de Ávila,(10) who was
captain of a supply-ship which had sailed far ahead of my gal-
leon, should be ignominiously put to death.

When I heard of this savage sentence I was ready to burst
with rage, and I called upon everyone to bear witness to the
great wrong that was being done to me, for I had served most
faithfully as could be proved in writing. The Duke heard
nothing of all this, for as I have said before he had withdrawn
to his cabin. Don Francisco de Bobadilla (11) was the man who
gave orders and countermanded them in the Armada, and every-
thing was managed by him and a few others whose exploits are
well known. He commanded me to be taken to the Judge Advo-
cate General's ship, and that whatever he thought fit should be

done with me. I went thither, and although the Judge Advocate, Martin de Aranda (12) *as he was called, was a stern man, he heard what I had to say and had private enquiries made regarding me, and thereupon found that I had served His Majesty well and as a brave soldier, for which reason he did not dare carry out on my person the order that had been given him. He therefore wrote to the Duke, saying that unless he sent him a written order signed by his own hand he would not carry it out, for he could find no guilt on my part, nor sufficient justification for it. At the same time I wrote a letter to the Duke which caused him to consider the matter well, and he replied to the Judge Advocate telling him not to carry out the sentence on me, but only on Don Cristóbal, who was hanged with the utmost cruelty and ignominy, although he was a gentleman and well known to many. God was pleased to deliver me because I was entirely guiltless, as you know well or will have been informed by many who witnessed these events, and the said Judge Advocate continued to show me favour out of respect for one who had right on his side.*

1.   de Cuellar is writing from Antwerp in October, 1589.

2.   The custom of including inexperienced men to accompany naval and military expeditions was not only a Spanish one. The youthful poet John Donne went with the Earl of Essex's forces to Cadiz in 1596, and to the Azores in 1597. The number of *Volunteers*, or Gentleman Adventurers, with the Armada is given first as 124 in the *Summary Statement of Vessels . . . collected in the Port of Lisbon . . . together with the Soldiers, Sailors, Pilots, Munitions, Provisions*, etc., dated May 9th, 1588. The number is increased to 254 by July 13th when the second *Statement* was taken at the *Muster at Coruña*. de Cuellar is here referring to the loss of *La Gerona* which affected him deeply. According to the Pilot General of the Armada, Marolin de Juan, there were only nine survivors from this wreck. These were not necessarily aristocrats but de Cuellar is not in general interested in the common soldier or sailor (C.S.P.S., pp. 285, 342 and 500). In reading his *Narrative* it must always be remembered that he was writing a private account,

not an accurate statistical report, and that most of the facts were of necessity based on hearsay only.

3. Note 'by the English'. The savagery of the Irish to those wrecked on their shores has been greatly exaggerated. Mattingly calls it a "myth" and states that it was fostered and "spread by the English almost from Armada year" (p. 311). It will be seen from repeated accounts in this tale that the Irish, unless they had thrown in their fortunes with the English, apart from taking clothing, jewellery and weapons which, like those in other countries, they considered their rightful perquisites, succoured and hid the shipwrecked men.

4. This seems a harsh word to use for the people who nursed and sheltered him. The Captain may have been of an ancient family accustomed to court and city life, associating with aristocrats and officers of what was then the strongest power in Europe. "Rough" or "wild people" might be as good a translation, but the word *savages* is also used by the English in maps of Ireland at this time, their accompanying illustrations showing the peasant people in rough homespun clothing in contrast to those of higher rank, and more stylish dress.

5. Spanish naval expeditions in the sixteenth century were looked upon as primarily military, the fighting forces being transported by despised sailors and galley slaves with oars. The Duke of Medina Sidonia always protested that he was a soldier, bearing the title of General, that he knew little of and hated the sea (since he was invariably ill), and that he was not the proper person to put in command.

6. The *San Pedro* who had been in the thick of the fighting in the battle off Calais Roads on Aug. 8th, 1588 (N.S.). She was one of the ten galleons of the Squadron of Castile, also styled "of the Indian Guard", under the leadership of Admiral, or General, Diego Flores de Valdés, a brilliant and ambitious officer, "one of the oldest and most experienced of the seamen" with the Armada. His name, together with that of his cousin who was his implacable enemy, is constantly given among the *State Papers Spanish* as one of those attending Councils of War called by the Duke of Medina

Sidonia. He had been ordered at King Philip's "suggestion" to go aboard the Duke's flagship, the *San Martín*, to act as his Chief of Staff, before the Armada had reached the English Channel.

The Galleons of Castile, together with those of Portugal—twenty great ships in two strong squadrons—were in the first line and therefore always in positions of danger and honour. They were intended to act in concert together. Those of Castile, to which the *San Pedro* belonged, were somewhat smaller than those of Portugal and less well armed, but they were "reinforced by four great ships normally in the West India trade" (Mattingly, p. 215).

The *San Pedro* is listed in the *Coruña Muster* on July 13th, as having a complement of 90 sailors and 184 soldiers, a total of 274. Earlier, in the muster at *Lisbon* on May 9th she was of 530 tons and carried 24 guns. Here she is given as third in the list and as having two less men on board—141 soldiers and 131 sailors. Six other galleons of this squadron were also of 530 tons, exceeded only by the flagship *San Cristobal* and the even larger *San Juan Bautista* of 750 tons. Two of the great merchantmen in this squadron exceeded this tonnage, making them even more unwieldy and likely to draw more water, the *Santa Catalina*'s tonnage being 882.

We hear of Diego Flores de Valdés and some of his ships in accounts of the battle off Calais and afterwards. One of his armed merchantmen went down in sight of both the English and the Spanish fleets off the treacherous banks of Zeeland, and in the solemn Council held aboard the *San Martín* after the battle in the Straits, and the escape from the Zeeland sands, when great officers, military and naval, disputed what desperate course should next be followed, it was Diego Flores de Valdés who was for making for Ireland, rather than for Norway, as Don Alonso de Leyva councilled.

7. The *San Mateo* was "a stout ship with a gallant captain", Don Diego de Pimentel, engaged in the van of the fight "somewhere off Dunnose", Isle of Wight. She was forced to drop back in place of a larger, stronger ship more heavily armed. Both royal

galleons were "in the post of danger and honour". On August 8th
at Calais Roads she was twice surrounded, "fighting a ring of
enemies . . . more than half her men were killed or disabled, her
great guns were useless and she was leaking like a sieve. . . . She
went on suffering broadside after broadside". Both galleons
eventually "turned aside and staggered towards the banks between Nieuport and Ostend where they went aground"
(Mattingly, pp. 256, 278, 283–4 and 286). About September 12th
(O.S.) a Portuguese sailor under *Examination* in Ireland reported
the loss of the two royal galleons, captured by the Zeelanders.

8.   Those familiar with El Greco's painting will know the "Death
of Count Orgaz". Don Diego had proudly refused to abandon
ship when the Spanish Almirante General had offered to take off
officers and crew. He was one of the prisoners to be interrogated,
and the Dutch later published a report of his *Examination* (Mattingly, pp. 284, 306).

9.   Both fleets were by now short of ammunition. At the
moment when it seemed to the English that they might finish
off the Armada before sunset a violent squall came up with
"blinding torrents of rain".

10.   A neighbour of Medina Sidonia's at San Lucar, and an
enemy, perhaps, over land or other problems at home. We do
not knowof the technicalities which made him the scapegoat.
He was "hanged at the yard-arm of a pinnace which paraded
through the fleet with its grisly burden" (Mattingly, p. 307).

11.   Or Bovadilla. He was Maestre Campo General, a position
exceeding that of the other camp-masters or colonels, obviously
a ruthless and much hated man. He had previously advised the
Duke about the inadvisability of sailing from Coruña because of
bad weather, and he and the Duke had had a disagreement off
Start Point (Mattingly, pp. 245, 314). He had had "many years
experience of fighting on land and sea . . . and had been ordered
by the Duke at Coruña to . . . go on board his flagship", where
the latter frequently took Don Francisco's advice (C.S.P.S.,
p. 403). On returning home he made a report to King Philip on
the defeat of the Armada.

12.   The Judge Advocate, or Auditor, "a Judge appointed to assist military or naval officers with his advice in law proceedings" (A/C, p. 47). The Count of Aranda had twenty officers submitted to him for his decisions and control, and the power of hanging the alleged delinquent captains. He appears to have been a merciful man since we hear of only one execution. It is not stated which his ship was—Spotswood-Green suggests *La Lavia* or *Labia*, Vice-Flagship of the Levantine Squadron.

> *I remained on board his ship, where we were all soon in imminent danger of death from a storm which arose, opening her seams so that the water flooded in hour by hour and we could not keep her drained with the pumps. We had no hope of safety nor remedy unless it came from God, for the Duke still failed to make an appearance and the whole Armada was so scattered by the storm that some ships were heading for Germany, others for the islands of Holland and Zealand (1) where they fell into enemy hands, others for Shetland, and yet others for Scotland where they sank or were set on fire. (2) More than twenty were lost on the shores of the kingdom of Ireland with all that was bravest and best of the Armada.(3)*
>
> *I was on board one of the Levantine ships, as I have said,(4) and two other very large ships came to sail beside us, to help us if they could. On board one of these was the camp-master Don Diego the hunchback,(5) and being unable to round Cape Clear (6) in Ireland because of strong head winds, he was forced to make for land with these three ships, which were very large as I have said, and anchor a little more than half a league from the shore, where we remained four days without provisions nor means of getting any. On the fifth day (7) such a great gale arose on our beam, with a sea running as high as heaven, that the cables could not stand the strain nor the sails be of any avail, and all three ships were driven onto a beach of fine sand with high cliffs on each side. I never saw the like, for in the space of one hour all three ships were broken to pieces and less than three hundred men escaped, more than a thousand being drowned,(8)*

among them many persons of importance, captains, gentlemen and others.

Don Diego Enriquez met his death in this place in the most miserable manner that ever was seen; out of fear of the huge seas which were breaking over the ships, he and the son of the Conde de Villafranca and two other Portuguese gentlemen, carrying with them more than 16,000 ducats' worth of jewels and coin, took to the ship's tender which had a covered deck, and went below, giving orders for the hatch to be battened down and caulked behind them. Thereupon some seventy survivors from the ship threw themselves onto the boat hoping to reach land in this way, but a great wave overwhelmed and sank her and swept them all away. Afterwards she drifted to and fro in the sea until she was cast ashore keel upwards, by which misfortune the gentlemen who had taken refuge under the deck died where they were. A day and a half after she had been driven ashore some savages found the boat, turned her over to get out the nails and iron fittings, and breaking open the hatch took out the dead men from inside. Don Diego breathed his last in their hands, whereupon they stripped him of his clothes, took all the jewels and money they had with them, and threw the bodies on the ground unburied. Because the circumstances are both extraordinary and undoubtedly true, I wished to relate them to you, so that you might know the manner of this gentleman's death;(9) but as it is right also that I should describe my own good fortune and how I came to reach land, I must tell you that I climbed to the highest part of the poop of my ship, and commending my soul to God and Our Lady gazed down at the great and terrible scene before me. Many were drowning inside their ships; others threw themselves into the sea and sank to the bottom never to reappear; others clutched rafts, barrels or floating timbers; others cried aloud from their ships imploring God to help them; captains threw their chains (10) and money into the sea; others were swept away by the waves, even from inside their ships. I gazed my fill of this fiesta,(11) not knowing what to do, nor what means of escape to try, for I cannot swim and the sea and wind were very *great. Moreover the land and beach were full of enemies dancing and leaping with delight at our misfortunes, and whenever one of us set foot on the shore two hundred savages and other enemies surrounded him and stripped him stark naked, handling him roughly and wounding him without pity.*

All this could be plainly seen from the wrecked ships, and the danger on one side seemed to me as great as that on the other.

I went to the Judge Advocate, God forgive him, who was very woebegone and miserable, and I told him to try and save his life before the ship went quite to pieces, and that she could not last more than a few minutes more—as in fact she did not. Most of her crew were already drowned or dead, including all the captains and officers, when I determined to seek my own safety and climbed onto a piece of the hull that had broken away; the Judge Advocate followed me, weighed down with the crown-pieces he carried sewn into his doublet and hose. But we could find no way of detaching the piece of the ship's side, as it was held fast by thick iron chains, and the waves and the loose timbers beating against it hurt us cruelly. I tried therefore to find another way to safety, which was to take hold of a hatch-door as big as a good-sized table which God in His mercy brought within my reach; but when I tried to climb onto it I sank some six fathoms under the water and swallowed so much that I came near to drowning. When I rose to the surface again I called to the Judge Advocate and helped him clamber on the hatch with me, but just as we were pushing off from the ship such a great sea broke over us that the Judge Advocate could hold on no longer and was swept away and drowned. He cried aloud to God as he drowned. I was unable to help him because now that the hatch had no weight on one side it began to overturn, and at the same instant a timber crushed my legs, but with a great effort I succeeded in keeping my place on my hatch, calling upon Our Lady of Ontañar (12) to save me. There came four great waves one after the other, and without knowing how I got there nor yet being able to swim I was cast onto the shore, where I arrived too weak to stand, covered with blood and grievously injured.

E

*The enemies and savages on the beach, who were stripping
any man who swam to shore, did not touch me nor come up to
me, seeing me as I have said with my legs and my hands and my
linen breeches smothered in blood; so I dragged myself away as
best I could little by little, passing many stark naked Spaniards
who had been left without a single garment and were shivering
with the cold, which was bitter at the time. And so when night
fell I threw myself down in a deserted place upon some rushes
on the ground, for I was suffering greatly from pain. Soon afterwards a handsome young man came up to me, mother-naked and
in such a state of terror that he could not speak or even tell me his
name. It must have been nine o'clock at night, the wind had
dropped and the sea was becoming calmer. I was soaked to the
skin and half dead with pain and hunger, when presently there
came by two men, one armed and the other with a great iron axe
in his hands; when they reached the place where I and my companion were we held our peace as if nothing were the matter,
and they were grieved at the sight of us, and without saying a
word cut a great many rushes and some grass and covered us
well. Then they went away to the shore to break open chests and
anything else they could find, in company with more than two
thousand savages and Englishmen from the neighbouring garrisons.(13)*

*I tried to take a little rest and did indeed fall asleep, but about
one o'clock I was wakened from deep slumber by a great noise of
horsemen, more than two hundred of them, hurrying to pillage
and destroy the ships. I turned and spoke to my companion to see
if he were asleep, and I found him dead to my great affliction and
sorrow. I learned afterwards that he was a person of some con-
sequence. There he lay on the ground among more than six
hundred other dead bodies cast up by the sea, and the ravens and
wolves (14) devoured them, for there was no one to bury any of
them, not even poor Don Diego Enuiquez.*

*When day dawned I began to make my way very slowly in
search of a monastery where I could recover from my injuries as
well as might be;(15) after great tribulation and suffering I*

1. With the English in chase after the battle in Calais Roads the Spaniards were driven by a persistent ill-favoured wind close in upon the treacherous shoals off Zeeland on August 9th. So ominous was the position of the entire fleet that they expected to be on the sands in less than half an hour. But the wind unexpectedly backed round the compass and the ships fled away north into the "Norway Sea", in spite of the Duke's and the Council's determination to do battle again. The reference to Germany is obscure. de Cuellar may have meant Friesland.

2. *El Gran Grifon* was the flagship of the *urcas*, or hulks, the tub-like freighters laden with wine and victuals, commanded by Juan Gomez de Medina. She was wrecked on Fair Isle with two other hulks off Scotland, and another two, were either wrecked or, being German, went off home. To a Spaniard the numerous Scottish islands were confusing and de Cuellar may simply be referring to one or more of them as "Scotland". The *Gran Grifon*, according to an English Captain reporting to the Lord Deputy in February, 1588-9, was "from Riske in Flanders". Her men escaped, reached Edinburgh and were to be shipped back to Spain through the agency of the Earl of Bothwell who "provided them with a double fly-boat of his own, riding now in the road of Leith".

3. de Cuellar here again refers to the wreck of the *Gerona* near the Giant's Causeway with Don Alonso de Leyva and castaways from two other ships, the remnants of his company, many of them of noble birth. It is possible that as many as 20 ships were lost off Ireland although all contemporary reports and later historians disagree. Mattingly accounts for 13 and admits a possible 17, giving the total Armada losses as 44 ships at most, perhaps a dozen less (p. 363). (Sir) Martin Hume suggests 17 in agreement with the Carew Papers. The *State Papers Spanish* grossly underestimate the number wrecked off Ireland since the informants depended entirely on word-of-mouth reports, sometimes hopelessly confused, sometimes wholly inaccurate. The Lord Deputy in Ireland gave the number "16, out of 59 seen, wrecked" in his report to the Privy Council, September 18th/28th, 1588, soon

after the Irish wrecks began to be noted (C.S.P.I., p. 41); Sir
Richard Byngham "16–17", on September 21st–November 1st.
(Ibid., pp. 48–9. See also Fenton to Burghley quoted later under
Streedagh.) Spotswood-Green goes as high as 25 from his own
investigations on the coasts.

4.   de Cuellar is referring to the nameless ship to which he was
transferred when in custody. The Levantine, or Italian, Squadron
of ships was commanded by Captain Martin de Bertondona. His
flagship was the great carrack *La Regazona*, the largest in the
Armada. The Levanters were armed merchantmen, or great-
ships in the second line of fighting, supplementing the galleons.
The ships of this squadron came from Venice, Ragusa, Genoa,
Sicily and Barcelona. The carracks had "lofty overhanging bow-
and-stern castles and deep holds: some of them were three-
deckers". Bertendona in the *Regazona* had been hotly engaged
off Portland Bill where he led the Spanish rearguard. The Vice-
Flagship was *La Lavia*, or *Labia*, on which it has been suggested
that the Judge Advocate sailed, together with his later complement of unhappy prisoners (Spotswood-Green, p. 443). The
ships of the entire Squadron were:

	Tons
La Regazona	1,249
La Lavia	728
La Rata Encoronada	820
San Juan de Sicilia	800
La Trinidad Valencera	1,100
La Anunciada	703
San Nicolas Prodaneli	834
La Juliana	860
Santa Maria de la Vison	666
La Trinidad de Scala	900

(C.S.P.S., pp. 282–3)

Out of the whole of this ill-starred squadron only one ship got
home—the Flagship, *La Regazona*. All the others were wrecked

or lost at sea—five of them on the Irish coasts, two more elsewhere, possibly off Ireland, "within the shelter of the Gola
islands". One can only draw the conclusion that the armed
merchantmen, whose gross tonnage was 7,705, were more
unwieldy than the galleons. de Cuellar distinctly says that, to the
ship on which he was, there "were attached two others, very
large—". Studying the fate of the other nine galleons in the
squadron (discounting the *Regazona* which we know got home,
and the *San Juan* of Castile which we shall see was wrecked with
the *Lavia*, and also *La Trinidad Valencera* and *La Rata* wrecked on
the Irish coasts elsewhere), this leaves five other ships as a possibility for the second in attendance on the *Lavia*, namely *La
Anunciada*, *San Nicolas Prodaneli*, *La Juliana*, *Santa Maria de la
Vison* and *La Trinidad de Scala*. *La Anunciada* was 25 tons less than
the *Lavia*, the *Santa Maria* even less, but the other three con-
siderably more, especially the *Trinidad de Scala*. Now the *Juliana*
is thought to have been lost in a bay just north of the island of
Aranmor, Co. Galway (Spotswood-Green, p. 446), although the
Pilot General of the Armada says that she "foundered on the high
sea, not a soul being saved from her" (C.S.P.S., p. 500). The
Anunciada is reported lost "off Ireland" in the incomplete list of
ships made by the Spanish (Ibid., p. 343): the *San Nicolas* and the
Santa Maria are also listed as lost herein, but not specifically off
Ireland; and of the fate of *La Trinidad* of this squadron no mention
is made. It therefore seems likely that the third of the ships
wrecked with de Cuellar was the *Anunciada*, *San Nicolas Prodaneli*
or the *Santa Maria de la Vison*—because of the tonnage more
likely one of the two first.

5. There were six camp-masters with the Armada, among them
two distinguished leaders of whom we shall hear more later—
Don Diego Enriquez and Don Alonso de Luzon. Each camp-
master commanded a company in addition to having general
control of his regiment (C.S.P.S., p. 284, note).

6. There are two Cape Clears, or Clares, off the Irish coasts—
one an island at the mouth of Clew Bay, south of Achill Island,
Mayo, the other north-east of the Fastnet Light and east of Mizen

Head, Cork. de Cuellar is referring to the first. Cape Clear was a major confusion in the Spanish mariners' and officers' minds. It seems never to have been pointed out to them that Erris Head was the spot to be avoided at all costs. But then it had never been intended that they should undertake this hazardous course. To the Spaniards all promontories were called Capes. Their name for Land's End was "Cape Longnose", and they spoke of "Cape Margate".

7.   This confirms the date for the wreck of the ship onto which de Cuellar had been transferred. The first mention of ships "cruising along the Sligo coast" comes on September 8th/18th when news of their sighting is passed on to the Lord Deputy in Dublin from Sir Richard Byngham, then at Athlone. His second, more definite, statement is forwarded on the 15th/25th—"three great ships have been cast away at Sligo" (C.S.P.I., pp. 29 and 41). He then wrote from Castle M'Garrat, Co. Mayo, about two miles south of Claremorris, on "Sunday morning". Presuming that the ships were wrecked before noon on the 15th/25th, word of mouth by a fast rider could reach Byngham on the same day. If we add to the 8th/18th two days for transmission of news to Athlone, four for the days when the ships rode at anchor, and the fifth for the day of the great storm and wrecks we again get the 15th/25th. (The usual period for news-in-transit from the west to Dublin in the east was four days.)

The three ships were wrecked on *Streedagh Strand*, a great crescent-shaped sweep of dunes and beaches lying near the hamlet of Milkhaven, north of Grange. (It is *not* the small stony strand marked by the authorities as Streedagh for the benefit of summer visitors.) Streedagh itself is difficult of access, even by foot, since the dunes in the close-on-400 years since the great gale have increased enormously.

As he surveyed the scene, contemplating his precipitous plunge into the boiling waters and probably into eternity, de Cuellar saw the sweeping arc of fine sand and what he calls "great rocks", or "cliffs". These are the Dartry mountains among which he was to take refuge. Outstanding among them is fabled Benbulben, which from certain seaward angles resembles the blunted prow of a ship.

Allingham reproduces a facsimile of an English Map of 1609— on which a rock called Carrig-na-Spaniagh is marked with a cross—as the exact place of the wrecks. But rocks with this name off Ireland, while perpetuating the approximate, do not always give the exact place of a wreck and should be noted with caution.

Buried in the high sand-dunes are the graves of prehistoric, probably Iron or Bronze Age, men. To stumble on these graves gives a kind of perspective to de Cuellar's plight, since there must have been many shipwrecks of men of many races here during the long centuries.

The sea-birds which frequent the strand are exquisite in their flight and movements—terns, oyster-catchers, gulls and flocks of wagtails who, true to their name of "dish-washers" or "lady dishers", dabble in and out of the clots of salt foam, chirping cheerfully, bobbing and bowing with their long elegant tails.

8.   Looking back on the holocausts of the September gales and wrecks Secretary Fenton is able to write to Burghley (Nov. 7th, 1588):

> At my late being at Sligo, I found both by view of eye and credible report that the number of men and ships perished upon these coasts was more than was advertised thither by the Lord Deputy and Council, for I numbered in one strand of less than five miles in length [Streedagh] above 1,100 dead corpses of men which the sea had driven upon the shore since the time of the advertisement, and as the country people told me the like was in other places, though not of like number. (C.S.P.I., p. 68.)

9.   There were two officers named Don Diego Enriquez with the Armada and—source of further confusion—there were no less than seven ships called *San Juan*, two *San Juan Bautistas*, and two *Maria Juans*. Don Diego Enriquez Tellez, or Tellez Enriquez, was the son of the Grand Commander of Alcantara, and Captain of the armed merchantman *San Juan de Sicilia* in the Levantine Squadron, accompanied by a relation(?) Don Pedro Enriquez.

In the battle of August 2nd the *San Juan* was in the thick of it and again, in that off Calais on the 8th, her Captain was commended for bravery, as well as the second Don Diego Enriquez, son of the Viceroy of Peru. It is *he* with whom we are here concerned. He, too, sailed on a *San Juan*, a galleon. When a consultation had been held on board ship by the Duke of Medina Sidonia at Coruña on July 20th, Don Diego was one of those questioned about the advisability of sailing: he had observed and remarked on the waxing of the moon and changes in the wind. Later, he was promoted successor to Pedro de Valdés as Admiral of the Andalusian Squadron. (C.S.P.S., pp. 348–9, 397, 441–5–8).

Nowhere in the *State Papers Spanish* is Don Diego Enriqez called "the hunchback", which would have lessened the confusion. As for the *San Juan de Sicilia*, the Rev. Spotswood-Green states that she was lost in the North Sea and Laughton that she probably foundered with the *San Matéo* and *San Felipe*, but it is just possible that she was in fact lost off the Blaskets. The Purser-in-Chief of the Armada, Pedro Coco Calderon, in an exceptionally long statement made at the command of the Duke, on September 24th when he had presumably reached Spain, says that on August 19th the fleet once more collected and they "looked anxiously for the *San Juan de Sicilia*, on board which was Don Diego Enriquez Tellez . . . She had been so much damaged that not a span of her sails was serviceable; and as we could not find her, it is feared she may be lost. . . . On the 22nd we discovered the main body of the Armada" (C.S.P.S., pp. 447 et seq). But the Levanters do not appear to have been present, and perhaps clinging together as a body they were wrecked off the coasts of Connacht when other ships blown south escaped and got home, or were wrecked elsewhere.

10.   There are several references to these in the *State Papers Ireland*. They evidently attracted the cupidity of both English and Irish, e.g. ". . . 16 of the company of that ship landed with chains of gold about their necks". Mayor of Waterford to Walsyngham (Sept. 23rd, 1588, C.S.P.I., p. 36).

11.   Translated by Crawford as "solemn occasion". The word

fiesta, (feast or holiday) may, however, also be used ironically to mean a "hullabaloo", or "riot", the nearest one can get to it in English.

12. For the significance of this supplication see pp. 40–1.

13. Allingham asserts that there was formerly a castle held by the English at Grange nearby—"an important outpost between Connacht and Tyrconnell where soldiers were stationed who used 'to sally forth scouring the neighbourhood for Spanish fugitives and plunder'" (p. 12). Today Grange is a plain little village on the main road north and south.

14. *Wolves.* "Wolves did not disappear from Ireland till the early part of the eighteenth century. There was a presentment for killing them in the county of Cork as late as 1710" (A/C, p. 51).

15. de Cuellar does not say that anyone told him where such a monastic house might be found, but being in a Catholic country he seems to have presumed that one could not be far distant.

reached it, but I found it deserted, the church and its images of saints burned, everything destroyed, and inside the church twelve Spaniards hanged there by the English Lutherans,(1) *who were prowling about searching for us and bent on making an end of all those who had escaped from the sea. All the monks had fled into the mountains in terror of their enemies, who would have put them to death also if they caught them, for this was their custom, as it was also to leave no shrine nor hermitage standing, but demolish them all or make them into drinking-troughs for cows and pigs. I am writing at such great length so that you may imagine the hazards and misfortunes that befell me, and so pass the time after dinner in the entertainment of reading this letter, which may well seem to have been taken from some book of knight-errantry.*

When I found no one in this monastery (2) *except the Spaniards hanging from the iron grilles of the church, I hastened outside and took a path that ran through a great wood, and going along it for about a mile I met with a rough savage woman, more than eighty years of age, who was driving five or six cows into the wood to hide them, so that the English quartered in her village should not take them. When she saw me she stood still, and realising who I must be said to me: "Thou Spain?" I made signs to her that this was so, and that I was one of those wrecked in the ships. She began to lament and weep much, indicating by signs that her house was hard by, but that I must not go there as there were many of the enemy in it who had been cutting the throats of many Spaniards. All this was terrible and afflicting news to me, alone as I was and suffering from my legs having been almost broken by a floating timber. But as a result of what the old woman told me, I decided at last to make for the shore, where the ships wrecked three days ago were lying, and whither parties of people were now hastening to cart away all our belongings to their huts. I did not dare show myself nor yet approach them, lest they should take the wretched linen garment from my back or even kill me, but presently I saw two poor Spanish soldiers coming towards me, as naked as the day they were born, crying aloud and calling on God to help them. One of them had a deep wound in the head, given him by those who stripped him naked. I called to them from my hiding-place, and they came to me and told me of the cruel murders and other punishments inflicted by the English on more than a hundred Spaniards they had taken prisoner. This was grievous news enough; but God gave me strength, and after commending myself to Him and His Blessed Mother I said to these two soldiers: "Let us go to the ships that are being plundered by these people; perhaps we may find something to eat or drink there." For I was in truth dying of hunger.*

On our way thither we began to find dead bodies, a sad and pitiful sight; they were still being cast up by the sea, and more than four hundred of them were lying stretched on the beach. We recognised some of them, among others the unlucky Don Diego Enriquez, and even in the sorry state I was in I could not pass him by without burying him in a hole which we dug in the sand at the water's edge; we placed him in it beside another worthy captain, a great friend of mine, and before we had finished bury-

ing them two hundred savages came up to see what we were doing. We told them by signs that we were burying these men because they were our brothers, and so that the ravens should not devour them; after which we went away and searched for something to eat on the shore, such as biscuits thrown up by the sea. Just then four savages came up to me, intending to strip the clothes from my back, but there was another of them who was sorry for me and made them go away when he saw them begin to ill-treat me; he must have been their leader, for they obeyed him. This man, by God's grace, protected me and my two companions; he took us away and remained in our company for some time, until he had set us on a road leading away from the shore to the village where he lived, telling us to wait for him there, and that he would return soon and direct us to a safe place.

To add to my misfortunes this road happened to be very stony, so that I could neither move nor put one foot in front of the other, for I was barefoot and in agonies of pain from a great wound in one of my legs. My poor companions were quite naked and freezing with the cold, which was very severe, and since they were more dead than alive and could afford me no help, they went on ahead while I stayed where I was, imploring God to have mercy on me. With His help I began to walk slowly along until I reached the top of a hill whence I could see some huts built of straw.(3) Advancing towards them along a valley, I entered a wood,(4) and had not gone further than the distance of two bow-shots (5) when out there came from behind some rocks an old savage, more than seventy years old, together with two young armed men, one English and one French, and an extremely beautiful young woman (6) of about twenty, all of whom were on their way to the shore for plunder.

When they saw me walking through the trees they turned in my direction, and the Englishman came up to me, saying: "Yield, cowardly Spaniard!", and slashed at me with his knife to kill me. I parried the blow with a stick I had in my hand, but he got at me in the end and cut the tendon of my right leg. He was making ready to strike me again, when the old savage came up with his daughter, who must have been this Englishman's sweetheart. I told him he could do what he wished with me, since ill-fortune had delivered me into his hands and my weapons had been swept away in the sea. Thereupon they forced him to leave me alone. The old man began stripping me as far as my shirt, beneath which I was wearing a gold chain worth more than a thousand reals;(7) when they saw this they were overjoyed, and began to pull my doublet to shreds, in which I had stowed forty-five crown-pieces that had been given me in Coruña(8) by the Duke's orders, for two months' pay. And when the Englishman saw that I possessed a chain and golden coins he wanted to make me prisoner for the ransom that would be offered for me, but I told him that I had nothing to give, that I was only a poor soldier and this money was what I had earned on board ship. The young woman was very sorry to see how badly they were treating me; she begged them to leave me my clothes and do me no further injury. Then they all went back to the old savage's hut, and I remained among the trees bleeding from the wound the English-man had given me. I set about putting on my doublet and coat again, but they had taken away my shirt and also some precious relics that I was carrying in a little vestment of the order of the Holy Trinity, which had been given me in Lisbon.(9) The young savage woman had taken these and hung them round her neck, making signs to me that she wished to keep them, and tell-ing me that she was a Christian, though she was no more a Christian than Mahomet was.(10)

They sent a boy from the hut bringing a poultice of herbs to put on my wound, as well as butter and milk and a piece of oaten bread to eat. I dressed my wound and ate, after which the boy came with me to show me the way, telling me to keep away from a village that could be seen from there, because many Spaniards had been killed there and none escaped who fell into their hands. For this good turn I had to thank the Frenchman, who had served as a soldier at Terceira,(11) and was sorry to see me so ill-treated. Before turning back, the boy told me to keep straight ahead towards some mountains(12) which appeared to be about six

1. His word for Protestants.

2. *Staad Abbey* (identified by Allingham) stands about two miles south-east of Streedagh Strand. (In Ireland ancient monastic cells, no matter how small, are called Abbeys.) The melancholy little building standing on raised ground close to the shore is now a roofless ruin. Only the east wall with a broken single-light window is left standing. The nave, and it is doubtful if it ever consisted of more than this although the Tourist Guide calls it "a portion of a small church", is filled with the stones of the fallen walls. These differ from those of the surrounding field-walls, round *carraigs* from the neighbouring strand, those of the Abbey being roughly hewn and cut, with some long stones for strengthening the building's corners. The whole measures 34 by 14½ feet. There are said to be traces of a much older building and this would agree with the Abbey's dedication to a Saint of the heroic age, the sixth-century Molaise (pronounced Molash).

So great was the fame of this saint that Columcille, when he had done wrong, placed himself under St. Molaise on the nearby island of Inishmurray, closely linked with the life, and perhaps the death and burial, of the latter.

Legends of St. Molaise still abound. In speaking with an old woman named Larit in a nearby cottage she told me that when the saint was forced to flee to Inishmurray, "he walked on the waters like Our Lord", adding "You can still see a green path on the waves sometimes where he walked. I didn't see it myself. Perhaps I wasn't there at the right time, and I'm not old enough myself to have seen him doing it!" The name of one of the Irish sailors with the Armada drowned at Streedagh was Cormac O'Larit (A/C., p. 10).

It is said that Elizabethan soldiers tried to burn his effigy, now in the National Museum, Dublin. Since the wood, seasoned by salt winds, was not easily consumed it was flung into the sea, but on the next tide, to the islanders' joy it was washed ashore. It is not of Spanish workmanship, nor has it any connection with the Armada as writers have asserted. But that de Cuellar may have seen it in the Abbey in which he took refuge, and from which he fled in horror, is possible.

Inland, towering over strand and abbey, stands the curiously-shaped limestone mountain Benbulben, with a flat top reminiscent of the greater African table-mountains. At its base are cultivated fields sloping gently upwards. These give way to steep rough pasturage vertically walled and speckled with sheep. Then, scoured with remarkable striations, the mountain seems to wear a ribbed collar, but any fancied head above it has been clean struck off.

This is the mountain associated centuries before de Cuellar's day with the mythical lovers Diarmuid and Grainnia and the ritual killing of Diarmuid by his enemy, Fionn, whose wife he had stolen away when placed by her under a *geis* which he could not forego—a bond of death and destruction. But Diarmuid was under an earlier compulsion, never to hunt the boar, and taking advantage of his knowledge of this Fionn lured him into a deathly chase. For it had been foretold that Diarmuid like Meleager would be killed by the wild boar's thrust.

Looking at what he calls 'high cliffs' de Cuellar may for an instant have been reminded of mountains known to him at home; but even in his own rock-bound country no stranger, more legend-haunted hill is to be found than Belbulben.

3. For a long time we have been assured by English writers that all the primitive Irish formerly lived in circular wattled huts, but archaeology and one's own eyes tell us that the people of different districts used, and still use different methods of construction. Estyn Evans, authority on rural Ireland, makes it clear that "stone, timber, wattle, clay, and sods were all employed from early times" in the making of houses, and that Ireland shared the traditions of the "timber provinces" of Northern Europe and the "stone province" of the Mediterranean. The dry stone-walling of the megalithic builders—of which there are more examples per acre in Ireland than in any other corner of Europe—continued on into relatively modern times, proves that the Irish were some of the finest handlers of stone in the world,

and in this they resemble their Celtic neighbours in west Cornwall. The thatch to which de Cuellar refers is generally today—
where it can be got—of rye straw, but it may also consist of tough
mountain grass, rushes, marram grass, flax, reeds, heather and
even potato haulms. de Cuellar does not mention the traditional
methods of pegging down the roof to the walls of the structures,
to prevent the gales from ripping it off; either with a net-
work of bog-fir, sally, or heather-ropes pegged into the thatch,
(or today with modern ropes tied to stone pegs at the eaves called
bachan), or weighted with hanging stones. Another common
method in the west was to plaster the ridge with mud (nowadays
with cement). The former kind of dwellings are known pic-
turesquely as 'stitched houses' and the latter as 'shaken' ones.
The mud-plastered type are still to be found occasionally in and
off the Mayo coast, through which de Cuellar wandered. In
Galway and Connemara another ancient method is to secure the
roof with hidden, bent withy-rods which peek out along the eaves
or at the ridge, a method known as the "scollop, or scobe thatch".
(Estyn Evans, *Irish Heritage, The Landscape, People and their Work*,
Dundalk, 1944, pp. 63-4.) We may, I think, see with de Cuellar
some of the simpler forms of construction described above,
cabins or houses, whether circular or rectangular, made from
local materials which melt into and blend with the mountains,
woods, and fields of which they are virtually part.

de Cuellar uses two expressions to describe the local dwellings
—*casinas de paja* and *casa pajizas*. In translating these and attempting to indicate the differences in the original manuscript Crawford
states that the former in his opinion means "huts not merely
thatched with straw but composed of it altogether", and the
second "thatched houses" (p. 43).

4.   The word in the original is *bosque*, "a thicket with under-
growth" in antithesis to de Cuellar's earlier use of *montes*, "a
larger wood" (A/C., p. 54, note).

5.   Bow or *harquebus*—an early type of portable gun first supported on some sort of rest, either a tripod, a trestle, or forked
carriage. In the sixteenth century it came to mean a "portable

firearm", and the OED gives 1594 as the earliest example of its use in English.

6.   "A very strong expression . . . consisting of a double superlative" (A/C., p. 54, note).

7.   *Reales*. Eight of these made a Spanish *peso*.

8.   Having sailed only so far as Coruña by "inchworm progress" and arriving there on June 19th the Armada was delayed for nearly five weeks. An epidemic had broken out among the men: there were leaking water-casks, needed ships' repairs, a shortage of water and bread, and to cap all a violent storm kept them in harbour and drove ships from their moorings. They finally set out again on July 22nd (Medina Sidonia to the King, July 25th. C.S.P.S., p. 354).

9.   From which the Armada had set out during the last week of April, 1588 . . . "now ready to sail, and only awaiting a fair wind" wrote King Philip to one of his ambassadors on April 24th (C.S.P.S., p. 273). On the 25th the Duke had collected from Lisbon Cathedral the blessed standard for the expedition "as an announcement that it was about to sail" (Mattingly, p. 190).

10.   Ireland escaped Roman and Saxon subjugation, and Christianity came to her two centuries before St. Patrick was sent to minister to the Christians already there. Owing to her isolation from direct Roman influence Ireland retained her own ecclesiastical, legal and social characteristics. Her "Christianity lagged behind in its original form, more Irish soon than Roman". (See Charles M. Garnier, *A Popular History of Ireland*, Cork, 1961, pp. 11 and 20 and N. K. Chadwick, *The Age of the Saints in the Early Celtic Church*, O.U.P., 1961, in which she describes Ireland as "an outlying province" and speaks of her being "the outermost ripple of the great monastic movement of the Greek and Coptic Churches of the East".) The Spanish church was closer to Rome, not only geographically.

11.   de Cuellar is here referring to either the 2nd or 3rd of the battles on the island of the same name, the "third" island of the Azores, during the period of Spanish subjugation, 1580–1640. The first battle, of Salga, was disastrous to the unauthorised attacking

St. Molaise
13th c. Carving in Irish Oak

BENBULBEN, CO. SLIGO

Spanish forces through the ingenuity of a priest who persuaded the islanders to let loose herds of wild bulls. Only 60 out of 600 Spaniards, it is said, survived. The second battle, of Villa Franca, took place a year later, in 1582, in which the Portuguese were aided by the French under Strozzi. But in 1583, under Santa Cruz, they were finally routed and the French fleet under du Chaste dispersed.

12. *Hacienda norte de las montañas:* The Spanish use the phrase metaphorically to mean "direction or guide", in allusion to the north star by which navigators guide themselves by direction of the mariner's compass. Strictly speaking the phrase means "the Arctic Pole". If translated "making for the north of the mounjains" this would give a wrong position for de Cuellar's hazardous tourney on foot (A/C., pp. 40 and 55).

leagues distant,(1) for beyond them there lay a good country belonging to a great savage chief who was a friend of the King of Spain, who gave shelter to any Spaniards who went to him and treated them well, and there were more than eighty men from our ships in his village, who had arrived there stark naked.

This news put a little heart into me, and with my stick in my hand I began making my way as best I could in the direction of the mountains, as the boy had told me. That same night I came to some huts where no harm befell me, for there chanced to be a man in one of them who understood Latin,(2) and so, by God's help in my hour of need, we were able to speak to one another in the Latin tongue. I told them the story of my misfortunes, and the one who spoke Latin took me into his hut for the night, and dressed my wounds and gave me supper and some straw to sleep on. In the middle of the night his father and brothers came home, laden with plunder and goods from our ships, but the old man was not displeased that I had been taken into his house and well-treated.

In the morning they gave me a horse and a boy to take me over the first mile of my road, which was very bad, with mud up to the girths. When we had gone the distance of a bow-shot along it

*we heard a very loud noise, and the boy said to me by signs:
"Save yourself, Spain"—for so they called us—"many sas-
senach horsemen are coming this way and will cut you in pieces
unless you hide. Follow me quickly!" They call the English
"sassenachs".([1]) He took me to some rugged clefts in the rocks
where we hid ourselves safely, out of sight of more than a hundred and fifty horsemen on their way back to the coast to rob and
murder any Spaniards they could find there. God delivered me
from them; and going on our way we met with more than forty
savages on foot, who wanted to cut me in pieces for they were all
Lutherans, but the boy who was with me prevented them by
telling them his master had taken me prisoner, and had sent me
on horseback to be cured of my wounds. But even this was not
enough to make them let me go in peace, for two of these ruffians
came up and gave me six crushing blows with their sticks on my
back and arms, and then stripped me of everything I had on me,
leaving me as naked as the day I was born. I speak the truth by
the holy baptism I then received. When I found myself in this
plight I gave thanks to God and prayed that His Divine Will
might be done, for this was what I truly desired. The boy the
savage had sent with me wished to return to his hut with the
horse, but he wept to see me stripped naked and so cruelly
treated in the bitter cold. I earnestly implored God to take me to
some place where I might die confessed and in His grace; then I
took heart somewhat, although I was suffering the extremest
misfortunes that man ever found himself in, and I covered my
body with a few fronds of bracken and a piece of old matting, to
protect myself from the cold as best I could.*

*Step by step, I went on my way towards the place that had
been pointed out to me, hoping to reach the territory of the chief
who had given shelter to Spaniards; and when I came to the
mountain range (3) that had been shown me as a landmark, I
found a lake (4) surrounded by about thirty huts, all of them
apparently deserted, and decided to spend the night there. Having
nowhere to go, I sought out the hut that seemed to afford the best*

[1] The phonetical pronunciation of the Gaelic word.

shelter for the night, for as I have said they were empty and deserted. Entering by the door, I saw that it was filled with sheaves of oats,(5) from which these savages make their daily bread; and I gave thanks to God for giving me so good a place to sleep; but just then I caught sight of three men at one side of the hut, all as naked as the day their mothers bore them, and they stood up and stared at me. I was somewhat afraid, for I thought they must certainly be devils, and they thought the same of me, wrapped as I was in my bracken and matting. They were trembling too much to say a word to me as I entered, nor did I to them, for I did not know who they might be and it was somewhat dark inside the hut. Such was my confusion of mind that I cried aloud: "Oh Mother of God, come to my aid and protect me from all evil!" When they realised that I spoke Spanish and was calling on the Mother of God, they too exclaimed: "May Our Lady be with us also!" Then I felt safe, and I went to them and asked if they were Spaniards. "That we are, for our sins; there were eleven of us who were stripped of everything on the seashore. We came naked as we are now in search of some land belonging to Christians; but on the way we met a party of the enemy, who killed eight of us, and the three who are here fled away through a wood so thick that they could not find us. That evening God provided us with these huts, and we stopped to rest in them, although there is no one in them nor anything to eat."

Then I told them to be of good cheer and trust always in the Lord, because not far away there was a land of friends and Christians; I said that I had news of a village some three or four leagues away belonging to the Señor de Ruerque,(6) where many of our shipwrecked Spaniards had taken refuge, and that in spite of my wounds and the ill-treatment I had suffered we would travel thither on the following day. The poor fellows rejoiced to hear this, and asked me who I was. I told them I was Captain Cuellar; they could not credit it for they believed I had been drowned, and they surrounded me and almost killed me with their embraces. One of them was an ensign and the other two

were private soldiers. Since my story is both comical and true,
as I am a Christian, I must tell you the remainder of it for your
amusement.

I buried myself deep in the straw, taking care not to damage
it or disturb its position, and after agreeing to rise early and start
on our journey, we fell asleep without any supper except for
blackberries and watercress. When in God's good time day
dawned, I was already wide awake with the terrible pain in my
legs. I heard voices and footsteps, and just at this moment a
savage came to the door with a halberd in his hand and began
to look over his oats, talking to himself the while. I held my
breath, as did my companions who had wakened also, and we
watched the savage closely through the straw to see what he
would do. By God's will he left the hut and went with many
others who had come with him to reap and work close to the huts,
in such a place that we could not go out without being seen.
There we stayed, buried alive, discussing what was best to be
done, and we agreed not to uncover ourselves nor move from the
spot while the heretic savages remained there, for they came

1.   The Spanish league is the same as the English; hence about
18 miles. It must be remembered throughout this narrative that
de Cuellar's measurements, since he was in a foreign land and
without means of verifying distances which the Irish gave him
by word of mouth, speaking in Gaelic or English, both strange
tongues to him, are only approximate.
2.   The first of two occasions on which de Cuellar mentions
Latin-speaking Gaels: the next time the man is a priest but here
we do not learn what rank the man had. There is corroboration
among the *State Papers Ireland* that Latin was not yet a dead
language in Ireland. One of the Irish princes in writing to Elizabeth used it; and on the island of Inishmurray there is a unique
gravestone with a Gaelic and Latin inscription, the Latin carved
in Gaelic lettering. The Irish were a nation of scholars when
much of Europe was under the hand of the Goth and Visigoth.
One may still hear tales from the Odyssey told round a fireside

in the west without a self-conscious sense of learning, or its acquisition, the tale being relished as it was among the Greeks of Homer's day for its own sake.

3. The Dartry, or Dartraigh, Mountains.

4. Lough Glenade, one of the smaller lakes in O'Rourke's country. The largest is Lough Allen, intersected by the powerful river Shannon, the uppermost of three great lakes thereabouts. Loughs Melvin, Gill and Glenade, in this order of size, lie in the northern part of his land, now known as Leitrim. There are many more enchanting lakes sprinkled about between the Dartry and Curlew, or Curlieu, Mountains to the south. Lough Glenade lies in the mountain pass (today a good road) leading up from Kinlough to Manorhamilton.

5. Oats, the great "corn crop" of Atlantic Europe, were probably introduced from Spain as long ago as the Bronze Age. Better adapted to damp than wheat, they became the staple crop for man and beast in Ireland and Highland Britain. Up to our own time in remote districts they were sown with a one-hand cast from a sack-cloth hung round the neck like a displaced sling. So precious were the oats they were often pressed down into the earth and covered over with a small hand-shovel.

Oaten straw was used for thatching or for fodder. Oatcakes cooked on iron or flagstone griddles, and then set on *harnen* stands of iron or stone, were for centuries the staple diet of both the Irish and Scottish peoples. A man would herd or plough all day at home with nothing more in his belly, and in harvest time a long draught of cooled oat-water was considered the most nourishing and refreshing of all drinks. When the Irish emigrated at the time of the Great Famine to America they took with them as much oat-cake as possible to keep them alive.

Anything so life-giving inevitably became linked with festivals and superstition. By the powerful Beltane hill-fires oatcakes which had not touched iron were consumed; bride and bridegroom were given platefulls of oats and salt on their way to the priest, and a cake of oatmeal was sometimes broken over the bride's head: while both meal and cake were a specific against the power of the evil *puccies* or fairies. *Sowens*, traditionally eaten at Hallowe'en, was made of soured oatmeal seeds sifted from the meal. (See Estyn Evans, pp. 8–172, passim.)

6. The 'savage' chieftain 'very friendly to the King of Spain' whom de Cuellar sought was Sir Brian O'Rourke, one of the most powerful leaders in Ireland (bar O'Neill and O'Donnell) descendant of the ancient Kings of Breffni. His territory lay to the south of the Leitrim mountains and included in it two "towns", one around his stronghold at Newtown (fragments of which may still be seen near a sixteenth-century castle), and the other at Glencar, on Lough Glenade. A map of the Great Lordships into which Ireland was divided eighty years before the Spaniards' arrival shows O'Rourke's country stretching from the sea at Streedagh inland far beyond Lough Allen, past what is now Carrick-on-Shannon, to the borders of County Longford. This was the Lordship known as West Breffni, half of the former Kingdom.

A sub-kingdom, Breffni, the "land of defence" and the "Rough Third", was part of the Kingdom of Connacht, protecting Connacht on the north-east from the rapacious men of Ulster. But it was difficult land to hold, and more difficult to gain, since it is in large measure mountain, desolate heathland and a tangle of lakes, some small and idyllic; others so large that it takes several hours (even with modern vehicles) to drive round their shores.

O'Rourke's ancestors had shown their pride and rejection of authority by slaughtering some of the monks of Kells in Meath which the O'Rourkes coveted and claimed; and again by attacking the retinue of the Archbishop of Armagh, killing his Grace's men in his presence, one of whom was the bearer of the sacred vessels. The most famous of them all was Tighernan, King of Breffni, a ruthless, proud, ambitious and vengeful man, whose wife was stolen from him by Dermot, King of Leinster, in 1152. Tighernan, whose chief fort was at Dromahair on the south-east shores of Lough Gill, now a scant ruin, like Fionn MacCumhaill relentlessly pursued his rival. Although he regained his beautiful and faithless wife—he died in 1146—her act brought ruin to

Ireland, for owing to Tighernan's descendants' persecution of Dermot, King of Leinster, the latter applied to Henry II for aid. Henry wisely refused but granted his Irish vassals the right to help themselves in what manner they thought profitable. Thereupon Dermot invited the "foreigners" to come over and aid him, and the barons of South Wales "invaded" Ireland in 1169. The Anglo-Normans established themselves at Wexford and the Norman invasion of Ireland, which brought more than 700 years of strife in its wake, began. In 1171 a succeeding Tighernan O'Rourke submitted in person to Henry II as he approached Dublin, but in spite of this submission he was slain by Norman de Lacy and his head set up over the gate of Dublin Castle.

Fiery by nature, and devout, the O'Rourkes of the earlier sixteenth century founded the Franciscan Abbey of Creevelea on their land, near an ancient church where St. Patrick himself is said to have worshipped. In 1570 and 1579 two O'Rourkes were martyred for their faith. Captain de Cuellar tells us that Sir Brian, to whom he gives the title of *Señor*, was a staunch upholder of the faith and this devotion, together with his refusal to submit to what he considered an alien law in his country, earned for him the enmity of the Elizabethan ministers of Her Majesty's justice.

We can follow his career in the *State Papers Ireland*. His bitterest enemy was Sir Richard Byngham, made Queen's Governor in Connacht about six weeks after de Cuellar's shipwreck. For his refusal to submit or give payment for his lands to Elizabeth's representative, unanimously hated and distrusted for his blood-thirsty treatment of the Irish, O'Rourke was constantly spied on and harried. Letters with information concerning him from Byngham to the Lord Deputy Fitzwylliam, from the latter to Burghley, from the Lord Deputy and Council to the Privy Council, and from subsidiaries to each in turn, multiplied and passed overland and across the Irish Sea. O'Rourke is not "coming to heel": he has combined with the petty chieftains to be kind to the wrecked Spaniards; "he hath let slip his son" to aid on the borders (an illegitimate son who escaped from his tutors at Oxford and got across to Ireland to aid his father): Lady O'Rourke (sister to the Earl of Clanricard) "is in Dublin suing earnestly the Lord Deputy not to place any sheriff in her husband's country, but her request has been refused": "an Irish friar is gone to O'Rourke with letters from the King of Spain, giving thanks for his service to the distressed ships of the Armada". . . . He is "daily visited with letters and messengers from all parts of Ireland". (Sir Richard Byngham to the Lord Deputy, Mar. 6th, 1588–9. C.S.P.I., p. 135.) On March 31st the Lord Deputy complains in more restrained language than Byngham's of "O'Rourke's waywardness": and a spy informs Walsyngham that O'Rourke has the temerity "to wish the Queen's sheriff [Byngham] appointed for his country to shift elsewhere for an office". In May, 1589, eight months after Captain de Cuellar's shipwreck, while he is still in hiding, O'Rourke is "preying, burning and spoiling" towns in County Sligo, on his borders, assisted by his clan and relations. Byngham retaliates by "persecuting them with fire and sword both by sea and land". In the same month the Lord Deputy reports from Drogheda that Sir R. Byngham complains that O'Rourke "had a long time been forborne, not for his deserts, but for some other respects". Towards the end of the month Byngham announces that, having with great difficulty got together men who would go against the rebels, he

> entered the rebels' fastnesses and marched all along their greatest mountains and drove them so from hill to hill as they durst not once abide our forces, but they having driven all their cattle so far up into their islands to the seasidewards we hit upon none of their prey.

(Ibid., pp. 188–9, from the "Camp at Conge", Mayo.) This driving by their owners of their cattle before them is something which de Cuellar speaks of later in his narrative.

Again in this month it is reported that O'Rourke is in league with one of the chieftains of the north, Sorley Boy O'Donnell, in order to obtain assistance from the Scots. He is (in June) "a sottish and cowardly traitor . . . the nurse and only stirrer", but for some unknown reason Byngham allows that his wife is "that honest woman . . . deceased in childbirth".

By September O'Rourke is "the verriest beggar and wretch" and in a letter to Burghley Byngham states that, together with another northern chieftain, he has "refused to deliver their Spaniards, notwithstanding the provincial proclamation". "He of all men lives most absolutely". The next complaint is that he has failed to come to the Lord Deputy at Roscommon. Byngham cannot contain himself and declares that O'Rourke is "that archtraitor . . . the nurse of all mischief . . . the most arranteste beggar: while this man is suffered to hold out, it will never be well in Connacht" (C.S.P.I., p. 209).

Goaded by all these complaints the Lord Deputy admits to Burghley in September that "O'Rourke must be chastised, otherwise he will continue a most noisesome neighbour to Roscommon and Sligo counties" (C.S.P.I., p. 242). Next, Byngham complains of O'Rourke's "proud terms".

A battle in the wet marshy lowland country in O'Rourke's land, in which O'Rourke's brother-in-law was fighting with the English against him, is vividly described—a fight in which the Irish Prince, knowing his own country "took the bog" and so escaped, but not without loss to his men (C.S.P.I., pp. 185–6, May, 1589). And so the desperate chronicle continues—he is supposed dead; he has fled to Tyrconnell; he is alleged to have made "suit into England to find grace upon a pretended submission" (C.S.P.I., p. 361, Aug. 20th, 1590), to Queen Elizabeth and her ministers. He has taken refuge with M'Swyne ne Doe (of whom more later) near Derry; he is "a traitor who ought to be plagued". He is "in miserable exile"; until Byngham triumphantly asserts that there "is not one rebel [left] standing out against the State in Connacht".

By now it is December, 1590, and de Cuellar has long since safely reached the continent, but his career and O'Rourke's are similar in one respect—that they both appealed to King James at the Scottish Court—and in vain. On February 24th, 1590–1, Byngham informs Burghley that "he has received information that the traitor O'Rourk [sic] has gone to Scotland to the Scottish court . . ." On March 13th Sir Brian's "flight is confirmed by a Scot, who met O'Rourke, accompanied by three men, repairing to the Court in Scotland". Fitzwylliam encloses a letter from one Byngham to another, written eleven days earlier, in which it is stated that O'Rourke has "gone to the King of Scots to desire him to be a mean [sic] to her Majesty for his pardon". So this is what is meant by the phrase in an earlier letter in which O'Rourke's "suit into England to find grace upon a pretended submission" is reported. In May of the next year Fitzwylliam is writing to Burghley about the latter's

> device to get O'Rourke delivered over to Her Majesty, as now I do hear he is. Withal you do require me myself and Sir Richard Byngham to advertise you of the particulars of his offence, and of the manner of the proceedings used against him and his son. Accordingly I have caused Edward White, Clerk of the Council of Connacht, to make an abstract of his misdemeanours and undutiful parts, which I send you hereinclosed . . . (C.S.P.I., pp. 393–4).

Proof of O'Rourke's "misdemeanours" is set down in a letter seized abroad, addressed to the Irish Archbishop of Tuam, then at Antwerp, five or six months after de Cuellar had found safe harbourage in the same city.

Having been, as the English put it, "nourished by" M'Swyne ne Doe in Tyrconnell, having passed over to the Scottish court, and having found no milk of human kindness in the breast of James VI who, being the son of his mother, the Queen of Scots, the Spanish and Irish still blindly believed could not fail to aid those who were of the same Faith, O'Rourke was finally delivered over to the English authorities. He considered himself a rightful Prince in the Kingdom of Ireland, fit to treat directly with Her Majesty, Elizabeth, scorning to deal with her inferiors who so grossly mishandled matters in Connacht and others of whom he was suspicious, thirsting for his blood. Fealty to the head of his clan, or to the Sovereign, was one of the basic Gaelic conceptions of rule and order, differing from the feudal Norman and Tudor conceptions, and to the Irishman negotiation by speech in personal audience has always been easier than through the written word or coded law. To the English, O'Rourke was merely one of the savage Irish who had not "come to heel". Arraigned for High Treason by the Grand Jury of Middlesex on November 2nd, 1591, his indictment and attainder were issued straightway.

O'Rourke pleaded for no mercy—only requesting that he be hanged with a halter of withy, as was the custom in his country, rather than with an English hempen cord. (Cox, *Hibernia Anglicana*, p. 399. This was also the Scottish custom.) On his way to the gallows the renegade Protestant Archbishop of Cashel, who had informed upon him earlier, endeavoured to make him recant. Brian, Prince of Breffni, scorned the Archbishop, reviling him for his own treachery to a greater than temporal power and so, proud and defiant, he passed triumphant to his death. (See A/C p. 24).

That O'Rourke was executed about Christmas time (1591), or early in the spring of the following year, is obvious from the melancholy assessment and parcelling out of his lands, "in order to reduce that country to obedience", which took almost a year (C.S.P.I., p. 457). Here he is referred to as "the last [late] O'Rourke": and in an entry in Jan., 1591–2, is referred to as "the executed traitor". His lands included five baronries three of which lay under the shadow of a mountain that divided the whole country into two parts: "the lands and grounds thereof are fruitful, though some bog and woods". It is these lands that de Cuellar took refuge in and wandered through for many painful winter months. The chief baronry of Dromohair, where O'Rourke's ancient castle stood, is listed as "most champaign ground and the best land in all the country". Then we come closer to de Cuellar's own ground—"the baronry of Roselougher [Rossclogher] is . . . a fast country" (by which the assessors meant wild, and secure against access or easy attack, a *fastness* as in Buck*fast*), "full of bogs and woods". The last of the five baronries is "champaign and very fruitful" (C.S.P.I., pp. 464–5).

The assessment closes with a recommendation that "All O'Rourke's places of strength *in islands*, loughs, etc. should be demolished or put into the hands of the English". This phrase is significant for what is to follow in de Cuellar's narrative, and the solitary hint that the Lord Deputy had personal knowledge, which he never admitted, of such "islands and loughs" and such "places of strength".

Connacht, the province in which O'Rourke's country lay and on whose wild shores de Cuellar had been wrecked, had been fortunate in previous decades in having two pacific administrators to effect the suggestions of the first—Sir Henry Sydney—for the adoption of the well-defined English system of land tenure, the establishment of districts or counties, and the appointment of sheriffs. But when Byngham took over, his harsh measures spoilt the good work of both Sydney and Sir John Perrott. Where before the people had been pacified and induced to adopt an alien manner of life, which in some ways bettered their lot, they now became restive and rebellious under the lash; Byngham was by nature cruel and bloodthirsty and scorning kindness as weakness he placed reliance on confiscations, breaches of faith, hangings and "puttings to the sword".

Government, as the English of the sixteenth century envisaged it, was foreign and unacceptable to the Irish Kings and their descendants. Double lords, and lords of a different kind, there could not be. One must make way for another or be destroyed, whether with honour or treachery, and in the records of the period treachery plays a revolting and terrifying part. The native governing Irish had for many centuries past looked in vain to the absent English sovereigns for just protection and support. Time and time again they had been disappointed. In the end they were forced to appeal to the military power of Spain or to the ecclesiastical authority of Rome. Scotland, too, was appealed to, since the clan rather than the feudal system of government still obtained there, and in the north and north-east of Ireland blood bonds were as close as the traditional.

Both the north and west of Ireland remained outside effective

English jurisdiction when the east, the south, and the rich middle lands had succumbed. Brehon law, tanistry, and other inherited customs prevailed, such as the service required by a greater chieftain from a lesser, and the right of the greater to levy contributions at will on the people under their rule. Men who worked for nothing were in return fed and cared for, together with their horses, dogs and cattle. Cattle- and horse-reaving, for long meritorious occupations on the Scottish and Welsh borderlands, and even in placid Somerset as late as the fifteenth century, continued in Ireland, and under the hated Byngham's tyranny became rampant.

O'Rourke is the epitome of a princely Irish leader of the old Gaelic order who, devout and courageous, like Homeric or Saxon heroes fought side by side with his friends, retainers and relations; who, embroiled in political and international affairs too complex for his comprehension, since he had never been educated or travelled abroad, defended his lands, people and faith with a wild and blind fury which could, as in some tragedy by Shakespeare or Webster result in only one thing—his own destruction. For the times were desperate, the wars merciless. The English were better armed, trained and disciplined. The mounted Irish rode without stirrups, using the spear and knife; the unmounted the axe, halberd, pike and short sword (while the English used stirrups and the short lance): they had few firearms and virtually no artillery unless sunken Spanish cannon which they salvaged from the shipwrecks or accepted as gifts from the Spaniards, whereas the English, well supplied, were enabled to besiege and swiftly take both castles and walled-towns. It was inevitable that the English should win in the long run. The Irish wars with England were a collision between two civilizations, two periods in history, two systems of government and warfare, two ideologies. That the Irish were forced to succumb eventually was a tragedy. O'Rourke's fate is in a manner symbolical, not only of that of many gallant Irishmen who did not submit to or ally themselves with the enemy, but also of that of the old Gaelic disunified nation itself.

from a place that had inflicted great cruelty on many of our poor Spaniards they had caught, and they would have done the same to us had they found us here with none but God to help us. Thus the whole day passed, and when night fell the treacherous wretches went away back to their villages; meanwhile we waited for the moon to rise, then wrapped ourselves in straw and hay against the bitter cold and left our dangerous hiding-place before daybreak.

We struggled through the mire, almost at our last gasp with hunger, thirst and pain; and by God's will we arrived at last at a place of comparative safety, where we found huts inhabited by people of a better sort, who although savages were Christians and charitable. One of these, seeing that I had been ill-treated and wounded, took me to his hut, where he and his wife and children dressed my wounds, nor would he let me go until he thought me strong enough to reach the village I was bound for.

In this village (1) I found more than seventy Spaniards, all going about naked and with injuries on their bodies, because the chief was not there, having gone away to defend a piece of his territory which the English had come to take from him. Although this chief is a savage,(2) he is a good Christian and an enemy of the heretics, and is always at war with them. He is called Señor de Ruerge [sic]. I reached his house with great difficulty, covered in straw and with a piece of matting tied round my body, so that everyone who saw me was moved to pity. Some of the savages gave me a rotten old blanket swarming with lice, and I covered myself with it and somewhat relieved my plight.

Next morning about twenty of us Spaniards went together to this Señor de Ruerque's house and asked them for the love of God to give us something to eat, and whilst we were begging they brought us news that there was a Spanish ship (3) off shore, and that she was very large and had come to fetch any Spaniards who had escaped. On hearing this news all twenty of us set off without more ado for the place where we were told the ship lay. We met with many hindrances on the way, and it was a blessing for me that by the grace of God I never reached the haven where

*she was, as did the others who were with me. For they embarked
in her, she being one of the Armada come thither in a great storm
with her mainmast and rigging badly damaged, and fearing lest
the enemy should set fire to her or damage her as was their constant endeavour, she set sail two days later with her crew and
those others taken from the land, only to run aground once more
on the same coast,(4) when more than two hundred men were
drowned, and any who swam ashore were seized by the English
and put to the sword. By God's mercy I was the only one of the
twenty who had gone to look for her who did not suffer the fate
of the rest. May He be eternally blessed for His most holy pity
and for all the mercies He has shown me.*

*As I was struggling along in great uncertainty and with much
toil, I chanced upon a path along which a priest was walking,
dressed in layman's clothes as is the custom of the clergy in that
country, so that the English shall not recognise them. He was
sorry for me and spoke to me in Latin, asking me what country
I came from, and for news of the wrecks. God gave me the
ability to answer all his questions in the same Latin tongue. He
was so pleased with me that he gave me some food he had with
him, and directed me how to get to a castle six leagues away,
which was strongly fortified and belonged to a native chieftain (5)
who was a very brave soldier and a great enemy of the Queen of
England and all that belonged to her, and would never obey her
nor pay her tribute, but kept to his castle and the mountains
guarding it.*

*I set out for this place, suffering many hardships on my way;
the greatest of these, and that which caused me most pain, was
that I met with a savage who took me by deceit to his hut in a
deserted valley,(6) and told me I must live there for the rest of
my life and he would teach me his trade, which was that of a
blacksmith. I knew not what answer to make him, nor did I dare
resist being put to work in the forge, therefore I showed him a
smiling face and worked at the bellows for more than eight days,
to the great satisfaction of the wicked blacksmith, for I was careful
not to displease him and the accursed old woman who was his*

wife. There I was, working at this miserable trade in affliction and sadness, when our Lord came to my help by causing the priest to return that way; he was amazed to see me there, forced to work for this savage who would not let me go. He berated the man soundly and told me not to despair, for he would speak to the chieftain of the castle I had been making for, and get him to send for me; this he did on the following day, sending four of his savage servants and a Spanish soldier, one of ten he had with him who had swum to shore. Seeing me half naked and covered in straw, he and all those with him were sorely grieved on my account, and even their womenfolk wept to see me so ill-used. They succoured me there as best they could, giving me a blanket such as they wore themselves, and for three months I lived there like one of the savages themselves.

My master's wife was beautiful in the extreme (7) and showed me much kindness. One day I was sitting in the sun with her and her female friends and relations; they asked me about Spain and other countries, and afterwards they begged me to look at their hands and read their fortunes. So there I was, thanking God that no worse had befallen me than to play the gypsy among savages. I began looking at the hands of each in turn, and telling them a thousand foolish things, which delighted them so much that none of the Spaniards was preferred to me, nor shown greater favour, and men and women pestered me from dawn to dusk to tell their fortunes, so that I found myself in a quandary, and was obliged to ask my master to let me leave the castle. This he would not do, but he gave orders that no one was to molest or trouble me.

It is the custom of these savages to live like wild beasts in the mountains, which are very rugged in that part of Ireland where we were wrecked. They live in huts made of straw; the men are robust, with well-formed limbs and features, and swift-footed as roe-deer. They eat only once a day and that at nightfall, their usual food being oaten bread and butter. They drink sour milk for lack of anything else; water they do not drink, though theirs is the best in the world. On feast days it is their custom to eat some half-cooked meat without bread or salt. They dress in

IRELAND, by ABRAHAM ORTELIUS
from his *Theatro de la Tierra Universal* (1588)

DRAVN AFTER THE QVICKE

Ashmolean Museum, Douce Collection

IRISH KERNES, OR LIGHT-ARMED FOOT SOLDIERS

1. Probably Newtown Castle near the eastern end of Lough Gill. (A neighbouring hill top is called "O'Rourke's Table".) To reach this would be a considerable journey for an injured man but no hint of leagues or miles is given, and Dromahair would be even further inland. That there should be as many as 70 Spaniards under O'Rourke's protection was a reason for agitation in the English governors' minds.

2. Here we get a clearer notion of what de Cuellar means by *salvaje*. Although he gives O'Rourke the courtesy title and rank of Señor he remains still, in de Cuellar's mind, a savage who lives in the wilds, unconnected with any visible court or monarch. It must be remembered that he never met Sir Brian. About this time O'Rourke was twice reported as having given arms to the Spaniards, as well as having written to those shipwrecked in the north to join him. Shortly before de Cuellar's shipwreck he had refused to give up the Spaniards in his keeping despite a pro-clamation. Three months later he is stated to be able to supply 500 horse and foot (C.S.P.I., pp. 49, 54, 232, 279 and 410). In the following May it is reported that 24 Spaniards are daily training his kerne—(light armed foot soldiers—the English definition is "one of the poorer class among the 'wild' Irish"): "they serve with pikes and armour such as was found in the country that remained of the last [late] Spanish fleet's furniture". In the month when de Cuellar sought his hospitality (October), the *State Papers* give no clue to where O'Rourke was. In December he was seeking a new wife whose father was called Iriel.

3 and 4. There are two Spanish ships involved here—*La Rata Encoronada*, and *La Duquesa Santa Ana* for which de Cuellar set out. The *Duquesa* was a hulk of the Andalusian Squadron under Pedro de Valdés. The hulks were Baltic ships, seaworthy, capa-cious, slow and clumsy, because of their shape resembling butter tubs or big-bellied cooking-pots, in fact Irish bastibles without legs. (The word *urca* in Spanish also means "a whale".) They were the nautical store-ships carrying essential supplies and their loss caused a serious drain on the fighting ships and men. The *Duquesa* was of 900 tons, 370 more than the *San Pedro* de Cuellar had set

out in: she carried a complement of 357 men, both soldiers and sailors, and had 23 guns (C.S.P.S., p. 281).

This was the second ship out of three on which Don Alonso de Leyva was wrecked. On September 16th or 17th (N.S.) the great carrack, *La Rata Encoronada*, dropped anchor in Blacksod Bay, north of Achill, south of the fatal Erris Head which the cartographers had failed to account for, and south again of Sligo Bay, in which de Cuellar was wrecked. The *Rata* chose an exposed anchorage off a small peninsula near Ballycroy. Soon afterwards another great ship, the *Duquesa Santa Ana* sailed into the same irregular bay and anchored off what the Elizabethans called Torrane, and the Irish today *Tirawn*, in Elly Bay—"the best anchorage in Blacksod" (Spotswood-Green, p. 440).

On the 21st the *Rata* dragged her anchor and was stranded. Yet another Spanish ship crept in but made no contact with the shore as she lacked a cock-boat, withdrawing out to sea again as soon as she could. By the 25th the fickle winds which wrecked de Cuellar backed once more to the south and south-west, blowing up into a *borrasca* of hurricane violence. The *Duquesa*, blown northwards, was wrecked further north in Loughross Mor Bay, Donegal. The towering cliffs here are of great geological complexity and geologists come from as far distant as Arabia to study their volcanic origins. Their general aspect is dark and forbidding and a single great rock, now detached from the headland's point, stands isolated, looking like a gigantic, stony barley-mow.

It is said that what appeared to be remains of the *Duquesa* might "still be seen when tides were low" and that one of her guns formerly lay "on an island in Kiltooris Lake" (Spotswood-Green, p. 141)—inland, east of Rossbeg. More recently amateur "digs" have been made at Kiltooris in the hope of finding treasure.

After the sinking of the great carrack *La Rata Sancta Maria Encoronada* which the English ignominiously called "The Rat", Don Alonso de Leyva, second in command of the entire Armada and a great favourite of King Philip's, gathered his wrecked survivors together and fortified them in an old fort, or *dun*, near the shore with the common name of Doona. The *Rata* was subsequently burnt. Rather than let her be taken by the English or Irish de Leyva gave orders for her destruction—de Cuellar implies that this was the Spaniards' custom—and she was burnt. Writing in 1906 Spotswood-Green says that traditions then still clung to the district of the wrecking of some nameless great ship from the Armada and he himself "secured one of her frame timbers of *Italian oak*, burnt off at one end" (p. 440). How close this description of the actual wood brings us to the lost ships, more suggestive of her origins, her building, and of the Spanish hardships off this relentless coast than golden coins, chains, or chests!

The wounded but undaunted commander then crossed Blacksod Bay with his company and joined the survivors of the *Duquesa*. Once more they fortified themselves in a ruined fort, at *Tirawn*, until they could plot their next move and take stock of supplies, ammunition and men. They set out in de Leyva's third ship, the *Gerona*, in which he was to find a watery grave off the Giant's Causeway, after a fearful journey on foot across the mountainous headland of Malin Mor—probably by the steep pass from Ardara to Killybegs cut by the Stragar River, beside which the road runs today. Either through hearsay or good fortune de Leyva found there the galleass *Gerona* and, with what remained of about 800 men from the two former wrecks he again entrenched himself, with men from the *Gerona* and two other wrecked ships in the bay. Taking planks from one of these they made the *Gerona* seaworthy, mending her rudder and making other essential repairs. On October 26th she put to sea with a company of 1,800 men, making for the "Out Isles of Scotland" (C.S.P.I., pp. 63–4). But although she successfully rounded Ireland's most northerly point she was doomed to disaster further east.

On the same day that the wreck of de Cuellar's nameless ship was reported, September 25th, the same informant tells us "The Spaniards, about 1,400, who were at *Torrane*, are gone to sea"

C.S.P.I., p. 41-2). This is a reference to de Leyva's departure from Blacksod Bay in his second ship the *Duquesa*—the very ship which de Cuellar had hoped to reach and from which he was saved by his injured leg. Another entry reads "the ship that was at Pollilly by *Torrane* [the *Duquesa*] has sailed, taking the company that was wrecked" [in *La Rata*]. There follows a list of names of Irish wreckers who "took out of the wreck [of *La Rata* before she was burnt] a boat-full of treasure, cloth of gold, velvet, etc. . . ." of little use to the "savages" unless they could barter it. . . . "He [de Leyva] departs for Tyrawley", that is the baronry of that name in County Mayo, one of the most desolate tracts in all Ireland, adjacent to Erris Head.

How did de Leyva depart? The terse notes made and sent forward with urgency need unravelling. Does it mean that he went on foot as he later did across another headland to Killybegs, or by sea? If we look at the map, and if we note the first informant's statement it must be by sea. de Leyva was therefore sailing round the dreaded Erris Head, making his way north after twice fortifying himself in ruined forts and twice taking to sea in two different ships, hoping to catch a favourable wind to take him and the men he had gathered together home to Spanish waters or, if too hard-pressed for water and victuals, to Scotland, where he hoped for more humanity than the English had allowed them in Ireland.

In the middle of these terse official statements there is a disclosure of larger import: *The Spaniards were commanded by the Pope not to harm Ireland.* Here is history in a nutshell. The statement can only mean because of Ireland's adherence to the Faith.

If you ask, in these patient unravellings of the *State Papers Ireland*, how do we know from the mention of anonymous ships which ship and which commander or survivor is being referred to, verification of the governor's, sheriff's, attorney's, or other English or Irish informant's tales may sometimes be checked with statements which occur much later in the *Spanish State Papers*— reports which of necessity came in weeks and sometimes months later as men crawled home overland by devious, interrupted

routes, or starving and half-dead by sea. Secondly—and these are
the most exciting and revealing of all sources—partial verification
is made from the so-called Examinations of survivors, whether
Irish, Flemish, Greek, Italian or Spanish; pursers, pilots, sailors
and soldiers, sometimes impressed men, sometimes willing adventurers, whom the English on apprehending examined, often under
torture, for we know from his commission that the Lord Deputy,
and no doubt the ruthless Byngham, were empowered to make
use of this (A/C., p. 22). As we shall see later when reading de
Cuellar's short reference to de Leyva's third and last shipwreck,
those examined have much to tell us, and in an intimate manner
which surpasses any historian's pronouncements. The survivors'
shorter Examinations, like de Cuellar's longer narrative, are the
rough fodder of history.

5. The second chieftain to whom de Cuellar was directed was
head of the clan of MacFhlnncdaha, Mac or M'Glannahie,
Glannough, Glannagh, Glancy and eventually Clancy, hence the
Spaniard's phonetical translation into his own tongue as *Manglana*.
M'Glannagh was a chieftain subject, as the Elizabethans put it,
"to O'Rourke's spending", in other words a lesser chieftain
bound to the greater's service. In the English assessment of
O'Rourke's lands made after his death it is stated that living on
them there are

> two sorts of freeholders—as the M'Glannoughs [and others].
> These pretend that they owe no service to Her Majesty but
> only to O'Rourke. The others are persons of inferior call-
> ing . . . (C.S.P.I., p. 464).

Listed as "one of the chief freeholders in this country" M'Glannagh is stated to be living "in the Dartry ·Mountains·"; and the
baronry of Rossclogher is given as "M'Glannough's country . . .
a fast country full of bogs and woods".

According to a local tradition, surviving as late as 1835,
M'Glannagh's territory stretched from Bunduff (north of
Streedagh) where the river Duff enters the sea, inland east to the
townland of Glack. It comprised in all about six miles in length

and three in width, and it lay on the seaboard side of O'Rourke's Breffni (A/C., pp. 15–16).

What M'Glannagh's lands lacked in size they gained in difficulty of access and hence strategic importance, for the district includes both high hills and lakes. The largest of these, Lough Melvin, curves like a gourd against the side of a mountain and is plentifully sprinkled with rocky islets. On one of these, Inniskeen, the clan had a lake-dwelling to which they resorted in times of danger. It may be that M'Glannagh was attempting to swim to Inniskeen when he was wounded in the arm and killed. Another of the islands was Rossclogher, which plays an important part in Captain de Cuellar's narrative. The castle of Rossclogher was one of two owned by the M'Glannaghs; the other Dun Carbery, or Cairbre (a ruined sixteenth-century castle) on a great rock nosing out over the surrounding meadows, bears the name of the fifth-century son of Niall of the Nine hostages. M'Glannagh's land was also rich in ecclesiastical foundations—the *termon* lands of three monastic houses.

This chieftain was a thorn in the Governor of Connacht's side. Together with O'Rourke, Maguire, and the powerful Burkes in Mayo he was reported in October 1588, as being "combined with the Spaniards". His kerne, joyfully attacking and burning, declared that they were "making way for King Philip". He gave orders that "all the wood-kerne", haunting the woods or wild country, "should resort unto him, and shall have entertainment", that is food and lodging. Secretary Fenton also reported that "the M'Glanoughes will not suffer our spies to pass" (C.S.P.I., pp. 28, 53–4). The letter was written from Sligo and it shows how the coastal road was then, as now, an important and necessary means for the passage of troops, stores and information. Again it is stated that this chieftain and his people "hinder espials reaching Ballyshannon"—the largest town in south Donegal, where the river Erne becomes tidal, famous for O'Donnell's Castle. In 1597, close on a decade after the Armada, the English suffered a disastrous defeat at the hands of the Irish and Scottish garrisoned here, many of them being drowned in the wide river-falls. Among the

Irish garrison there were six Spaniards, survivors of the Armada who had somehow miraculously escaped detection, imprisonment or death.

M'Glannagh, like O'Rourke, fell to the English. At the end of April 1590, Byngham writes to the Lord Deputy, with obvious relish:

M'Glannaghe's head brought in. M'Glannaghe ran for a loch which was near, and tried to save himself by swimming, but a shot broke his arm, and a gallowglass [one of a particular class of soldiers or retainers formerly maintained by Irish chieftains] brought him ashore. He was the best killed man in Connaught a long time. He was the most barbarous creature in Ireland, and had always 100 knaves about him. He would never come before any officer. His country extended from the Grange beyond Sligo till you come to Ballyshannon. He was O'Rourke's right hand. He had 14 Spaniards, some of whom were taken alive.

The letter was enclosed with one from Sir Richard to Burghley in which he speaks of

the acceptable service performed by Sir George Byngham in cutting off, on Good Friday last, M'Glannaghe, an arch-rebel, who never lived dutifully one day in all his life, but did prey, steal, and commit murders on the borders of Sligo, and never paid her Majesty one penny of rent for all the lands in his country. (C.S.P.I., pp. 333.)

O'Rourke thereby lost his "right hand" man and M'Glannagh's capture and killing may have been the immediate cause of O'Rourke's journey to Scotland to negotiate with the King. Had de Cuellar stayed in hiding with either O'Rourke or M'Glannagh, among the Darty or Leitrim mountains, he too would very likely have been apprehended and killed.

In 1586, two years before the arrival of the distressed Armada ships off the Irish coasts, an extraordinary act of disrespect to the Virgin Queen, a primitive and public symbolical ceremony, took place in M'Glannagh's country, in one of his "towns", possibly Kinlough. It was witnessed by an Englishman, a Mr.

John Ball, who was sent into O'Rourke's country "to receive Her Majesty's composition". He appears to have been a serious, humourless man, but he did his duty in reporting the ceremony. Five weeks after doing so he was questioned by the under-sheriff of the province, and the presence of the mysterious effigy was duly reported to Byngham, then to the Lord Deputy, and so on to Burghley. Mr. Ball stated:

> In the time of my being there, at M'Glannagh's town, stand-ing upon a green, I saw the picture [image] of a woman carved in a block, standing upon wheels of small timber. I asked the inhabitants of the town what it was. They told me it was made for a calliagh [an evening merrymaking]. I asked who she was. They told me one that denied a carpenter of milk. I demanded where she did dwell. They said on the far side of the water. By the town there was a lough. I thought they meant on the far side thereof, and so said no more of that. (C.S.P.I., p. 122.)

The effigy was insulted and possibly later burnt, as the Porgu-guese "in their holy house in Lisbon" in a fury burnt "their holy woman" on hearing of the defeat of the Armada (C.S.P.I., p. 336), and as children today burn Guy Fawkes.

There are five more references to the wooden effigy in the *State Papers* in the ensuing five years. Since its existence in O'Rourke's sub-territory, and his alleged knowledge of it, were produced as evidence at his trial and indictment for high treason (*Note of the Charges against O'Rourke*, about November, 1591, C.S.P.I., p. 440), it is worth quoting the most vivid of the descriptions of the mutilation of this stolen figure. In reading it one should consider that M'Glannagh was the lesser chieftain for whose actions O'Rourke, the greater, was responsible. O'Rourke himself may never have seen the wooden effigy which Mr. Ball states was in M'Glannagh's "town". It will be seen that the Lord Deputy, writing to Burghley, was at pains to contradict rumours against Byngham that he had falsely lured O'Rourke with "fair speeches and promises", and that the latter was forced to flee for his life.

O'Rourke, about two or three years since, having found in a church or some other place an image of a tall woman wrote upon the breast thereof *Queen Elizabeth*, which done he presently fell with such spiteful and traitorous speeches to rail at it, and otherwise so filthily to use it, as I protest unto your Lordship [William Cecil, Baron Burghley, Lord High Treasurer, and Chief Minister of Queen Elizabeth] I abhor to remember, and can by no means frame my pen to write. During which time his barbarous gallowglasses standing by played their parts as fast, who with their gallowglass axes striking the image one while on the head, another while on the face, and sometimes stabbing it in the body, never ceased until with hacking and mangling they had utterly defaced it. And being nevertheless not contented herewith they, the more to manifest the malice of their traitorous hearts, fastened a halter about the neck of the image, and tying it to a horse-tail dragged it along upon the ground, and so beating it with their axes, and railing most despitefully at it they finished their traitorous pageant.

The report hereof soon after being brought to Sir Richard Bingham, he not being able to endure that so savage a traitor should live, secretly one night taking his footband with him marched towards O'Rourke, intending before he could have had notice thereof suddenly to have surprised him in his house, being situate on a plot of ground environed about with a great lough. But good endeavours have not ever best success. It happened that Sir Richard with his company being approached near to the lough side, they were through the brightness of the night by reason of a great fall of snow, discovered by some of O'Rourke's servants, who presently raised the cry; O'Rourke thereupon suspecting that somebody was coming leapt into a boat on the other side of the lough, and fled away into the woods and fastness of his country. This is the truth and circumstances of O'Rourke's flying away in a boat. (C.S.P.I., pp. 142–3.)

6. Either the Glenade or Glencar Valley, between which the Dartry Mountains lie—their finest summits being Truskmore, King's Mountain, and Benbulben jutting out seawards. The

scenery here is tropical in its luxuriance, like that of west Kerry. The arbutus blooms in the same profusion, and over all there is a soft Lombardian light.

7. A slight modification in superlatives from the phrase used previously to describe the Irish women in general.

tight hose and short coats of coarse goat's hair; over this they wear a blanket (1) and their hair falls low over their eyes. They are good walkers and hard workers. They are constantly at war with the English from the Queen's garrisons near by, defending themselves from them, and refusing to let them enter their territory, all of which is liable to flood and covered in swamps. This district measures in all more than forty leagues square. Their greatest desire is to be thieves and plunder one another, so that hardly a day passes without a call to arms among them, for as soon as the men of one village discover that there are cattle or anything else in another village they come armed by night, and attack (2) and kill each other. The English garrisons get to know who has rounded up and stolen most cattle, and at once fall upon them and take away their spoils, leaving them with no remedy but to retreat into their mountains with their women and cattle, for they possess no other property, neither furniture nor clothing. They sleep on the ground on freshly cut rushes, full of water and ice. Most of the women are very beautiful but poorly dressed; they wear nothing but a smock covered with a blanket, and a linen kerchief folded tightly round their heads and fastened in front. They are hard workers and good housewives after their fashion. These people call themselves Christians; they say Mass among themselves and observe the rituals of the Church of Rome, but nearly all their churches, monasteries and hermitages have been demolished by the English garrisons and by those of the natives who have joined them and are as bad as they are. In short there is neither justice nor order in this country and every man does exactly as he pleases.(3)

These savages liked us Spaniards well; because they knew we had come to fight the heretics and were their deadly enemies;

indeed if they had not taken as much care of us as they did of themselves not one of us would still be alive. We were grateful to them for this, although they had been the first to rob and strip naked any man cast alive on their shores, from whom these savages gained great wealth in jewels and money, as they did also from the thirteen ships of our Armada with many important people on board, all of whom were drowned.

The news of this having reached the Queen's Lord Deputy in the city of Dublin,(4) he at once set forth with seventeen hundred soldiers to look for the wrecked ships and any men who had escaped from them, of whom nearly a thousand must have been wandering naked and unarmed in those parts of the country where the ships had been wrecked. The Lord Deputy caught many of them and immediately hanged them or inflicted other penalties on them, and anyone who was known to have sheltered our men was put in prison (5) and maltreated in every possible way, insomuch that he seized upon three or four savage chiefs who had taken some Spaniards into their castles, put both parties under arrest and marched with them along the shore as far as the place where I had been wrecked.(6) From there he turned off towards the castle of Manglana, (7) for so the savage with whom I was living was called. He had always been a bitter enemy to the Queen, and he neither loved anything that was hers nor was willing to obey her, for which reason the Lord Deputy desired to take him prisoner. But seeing the great force advancing towards him, and having no power to resist it, the chief decided to fly into the mountains, which were his only remaining refuge.

We Spaniards who were living with him had already heard news of our approaching danger, and knew not what to do nor where to go for safety. One Sunday after Mass the chief took us on one side, and with his hair over his eyes and in a furious rage told us that he could stay there no longer, that he had decided to fly with all his people, their cattle and families, and that we must consider what to do to save our lives. I replied begging him to calm himself a little, and saying that we would give him our answer immediately. Then I went aside with the eight Spaniards *who were with me, good fellows all, and told them to think well over all our past troubles and the danger which was now threatening us, and consider whether it would not be better to make an honourable end of it all, lest worse should befall; we now had an excellent opportunity, and there would be no need to wait any longer, nor to take to our heels among the mountains and woods, naked and barefoot in this bitter cold. Since the native chieftain was so loth to leave his castle unprotected, we nine Spaniards would gladly remain in it and defend it with our lives; this we could do very well, even if twice as many more should attack it as were now approaching, because the castle was extremely strong and very difficult to storm without artillery, for it was built in the middle of a very deep lake,(8) more than a league across in some places and three or four leagues long, with an outlet to the sea. Even during the spring tides there was no means of entry that way, so that the castle could not be taken either from the water or from the nearest strip of land, nor could it be damaged, because for a space of one league all round the town (which is built on the mainland) there is a swamp, breast-deep, so that even the inhabitants can only reach it by footpaths.(9)*

After considering all this carefully, we decided to tell the native chief that we would defend his castle to the death, and ask him to supply it with provisions for six months and some arms with all speed.(10) The chief was so pleased with our reply, and at finding us so full of courage, that he lost no time in provisioning the castle, with the full approval of the principal men of the town, who were all well satisfied. And to ensure that we should not play him false, he made us swear that we would not abandon his castle, nor surrender it to the enemy by means of any treaty or covenant even if we were dying of hunger, nor yet open the gates and allow any Irishman, Spaniard or other person to enter before he himself had returned, as he would without fail. After all necessary preparations had been made we posted ourselves in the castle, taking with us the ornaments and furnishings from the church and one or two relics that were there; we took in also two or three boat-loads of stones, together with six muskets, six

1. When Sir William Herbert inveighed against Irish customs and habits, in an attempt to make the country people live a more "loyal, dutiful and civil life", he wrote that:

The mantle serving unto the Irish [is] as to a hedgehog his skin, or to a snail her shell, for a garment by day and a house by night: it maketh them, with the continual use of it, more apt and able to live and lie out in bogs and woods, where their mantle serveth them for a mattress and a bush for a bedstead. (C.S.P.I., pp. 192–3.)

2. *anda Santiago:* a slang expression derived from the name of the patron saint of Spain. A war-cry on going into action.

3. This paragraph has been quoted by one historian of Ireland as showing the degradation to which the Irish people had descended after "four centuries of unsuccessful English conquest. . . ."

They were refused all means of protecting themselves: they were hunted as an inferior race: the good elements which we can glimpse from the deposition of de Cuellar, such as the women, were deliberately ruined. The disorder was as great among the long established English . . . (Charles-M. Garnier, *A Popular History of Ireland*, p. 54, Cork, 1961.)

M. Garnier is just about the persistent failure in systems of government attempted in Ireland throughout the centuries preceding and during the Armada periods, but I do not feel that de Cuellar meant to, or does prove the degradation in the way of life of these pastoral people.

That they only ate one meal a day is no proof that they could not have eaten more had they so wished. It is still the custom of some old people in the west to eat but one meal. I have known fishermen refuse food offered them on the grounds that "this eating is only a fashion", and it is well known that Scottish shepherds who walk many miles in their day's work survive on a single meal of porridge or oatcake. Tomas O'Crohan in *The Islandman* and Maurice O'Sullivan in *Twenty Years a-Growing* both tell of men gathering heavy driftwood, seal-catching, or fishing by night, who went twenty-four hours without anything to eat or drink, being none the worse for it.

Clothing spun from sheep's wool and formerly goat's hair has long been the customary clothing of mountainous or highland people in Ireland, Wales and Scotland, the natural oils retained in the wool keeping out mist and rain. As for furniture and possessions few of these have ever been the treasured objects of peasant peoples except those of necessity. The "living-room" of a well-kept and well-off home in the west of Ireland today sometimes contains little more than a family dresser, a settle, a wooden table (a relatively modern innovation), a couple of hard chairs, the "ware" on the dresser, and the iron kettle and cooking-pot by the turf fire. The hearth has always been the focal point of family life and most domestic utensils are either for cooking or milking, since hospitality to the stranger and neighbour, and the pastoral life, were and still are the basis for Irish rural life. Rushes are mentioned by Estyn Evans as being used for "floor-beds".

It must not be forgotten that de Cuellar, a Spaniard of the 'upper' class, is describing the Irish as he found them. His impressions and attitude were necessarily coloured by his memories of, and customs in his own country—one of the most ancient and civilized in Europe, then at the height of her power, with vast territories in three continents.

4. Sir William Fitzwylliam (1526–99), Lord Deputy of Ireland. Although a Protestant he had supported Mary Tudor. Given the unpleasant task of being the guardian of Mary, Queen of Scots, when imprisoned in Fotheringay Castle, of which he was Governor, he appears to have won her respect since she gave him before her execution a portrait of her son, James. Vice-Treasurer in Ireland (1559–73) and Lord Justice (1571) he was made Lord Deputy (1572–5) and reappointed to this office (1588) when he made his expedition, herein referred to, into Connacht. Having pacified Monaghan and suppressed Maguire in Cavan he left Ireland in 1599, the year in which he died. He certifies that he was "a full 63" when he made his journey into Connacht, in a

time of year unheard of "in the memory of man"—November
and December of 1588. He writes to Burghley next April that
"his memory is weak, his body so unwieldy that he can not walk
on his legs without grief, or get up but by a stool". On October
12th/22nd he asked for three or four ships and 2,000 men—
"sufficient and thoroughly well-appointed, and so many more
after as speedily as your Lordships shall deem this dangerous time
and service to require"—to suppress a possible rising in the north-
west in O'Donnell's country, that is in Donegal. Sir William
feared that the Irish might unite with the Spaniards and the Scots,
whereupon he presumed that "the most of the English Pale and
towns will make revolt, and other hope we can have none"
(C.S.P.I., p. 53).

The Lord Deputy set out through Connacht into M'Sweeny
ne Doe's country (N. Western Donegal) intending to return
through that of O'Donnell and O'Neill, the Earl of Tyrone.
Wallop writing to Walsyngham on November 7th/17th prophesied that he might find few Spaniards left in the north by the
time he reached it, some being fled into Scotland, "and so
shorten his journey" (C.S.P.I., p. 72). Byngham makes another
spiteful reference to his march on December 3rd/13th, 1588.
But it is what the Lord Deputy himself writes in between his
long marches that is of prime importance. By November 10th/
20th he had reached Athlone, a stage of seventy-eight modern
English miles—the Cromwellian Irish are longer—from Dublin.
He writes to Burghley:

I at this present with her Majesty's army am entered into it
[the journey into the west and north] as far as Athlone;
wherein, if either the deepness of winter, which yieldeth
short days and long nights, foul ways, great waters, many
stormy showers, want of horsemeat, hazard of spoiling, and
loss both of horses and garans [small horses or native ponies]
which have our carriages, besides the report that there were
not above one hundred or thereabouts left of the ragged
Spaniards would have persuaded me to stay, I should not
have gone forwards. Every man has a liking to the journey.

The Irish fearing my approach put the Spaniards away . . . (C.S.P.I., pp. 74 and 77.)

By November 24th/December 4th Fitzwylliam has reached Ballyshannon, the important post at the mouth of the Erne, 140 miles distant from Dublin, where he is proceeding "against the remains of Spaniards"

> left straggling in the north parts of this realm, who I understand are in number 4 or 500 dispersed in poor estate into divers parts, and yet so favoured and succoured by the country people, as it will be hard to hunt them out, but with long time and great labour. (C.S.P.I., p. 76.)

By December 31st/January 10th Fitzwylliam had returned to Dublin and reports (with others) to the Privy Council in England in a letter of unusual length—six and a half foolscap pages:

> Now I have thought meet to acquaint [your Lordships] with some particularities concerning the said journey . . . I undertook the journey the 4th of November and finished the same the 23rd of this instant December, being seven weeks and one day, returning without loss of anyone of Her Majesty's army, neither brought I home, as the captains informed me, scarce 20 sick persons or thereabouts, neither found I the waters nor other great impediments, which were objected before my going out to have been most dangerous, otherwise than very reasonable to pass. (C.S.P.I., p. 92 et seq.)

He then goes on to write about Don Alonso de Leyva, with whom we shall be concerned later. After this Fitzwylliam recapitulates and goes on to speak of the country in which O'Rourke, M'Glannagh and de Cuellar were.

> I took my journey from Dublin directly to Athlone and from thence through Connaught to Sligo, where Her Majesty's army from Munster Leinster and those of Connaught met together. . . . As I passed from Sligo, having then gone 120 miles, I held on towards Bundrowes [Leitrim and O'Rourke's country] and so to Ballyshannon the uttermost part of Connaught that way . . . and riding still along

ROSSCLOGHER CASTLE, CO. LEITRIM

THE CLIFFS OF MOHER, CO. CLARE

the sea coast I went to see the bay where some of those ships
wrecked [Streedagh strand], and where, as I heard, lay not long
before 1,200 or 1,300 of the dead bodies [of the Spaniards].
I rode along upon that strand near two miles (but left behind
me a long mile or more), and then turned off from that shore,
leaving before me "a mile and better's riding", in both which
places they said that had seen it, there lay as great store of the
timber of wrecked ships as was in that place which myself
had viewed, being in mine opinion ... more than would
have built five of the greatest ships that ever I saw, besides
mighty great boats, cables and other cordage answerable
thereunto, and some such masts for bigness and length, as in
mine own judgement I never saw any two could make the
like.

At my coming to the castles of Ballyshannon and Beleek,
which stand upon the river of Erne ... I found all the
country and cattle fled into the strong mountains and fastness
of the woods in their own countries and neighbours' adjoin-
ing, as to O'Rourke, O'Hara, the M'Glannaghies, Maguire
and others. And so I found until I came to Donegal ...

After a further two and a half pages Sir William thanks their
lordships and Her Majesty for the despatch thither of

men, munition and money ... most humbly beseeching
your favourable remembrance for a greater portion; for that
the soldiers' month's victualling money and a month's
imprest being given to every of the bands, which is with the
least, considering their great want and poor estate before this
journey, wherein they have in the cold season of winter
marched 320 and odd miles, and therefore greatly needful to
be refreshed. ...

Two pages later he closes on what, but for good fortune and
his able watchfulness, might have been a major disaster for the
English crown. He speaks first of several letters written by Don
Alonso de Leyva before his final wreck, letters

sent away by special men into Spain, but whether directly
from hence or through Scotland, I cannot find out. Only it

may please you that if . . . there had been but 1,000 men with victuals and powder, of both which he was unfurnished, sent him out of Spain, to have assisted him and his 2,600 men, which now are all rid hence, I see not how but that before I could have given your Lordships advertisement, Her Majesty *might have been dispossessed of Ireland*. (C.S.P.I., pp. 92–8, italics mine.)

5.   Byngham, in protest, reports to the Queen on December 3rd (O.S.) that

The men of these [wrecked] ships all perished, save 1,100 or more who were put to the sword [not by the Lord Deputy] amongst whom were officers and gentlemen of quality to the number of 50. . . . These gentlemen were spared till the Lord Deputy sent me special direction to see them executed, as the rest were only reserving alive one Lewes de Cordova and his nephew until your Majesty's pleasure be known. . . . My brother George . . . had one Don Graveillo de Swasso and another gentleman by licence, and some five or six Dutch boys and young men, who coming after the fury and heat of justice were passed, by entreaty I spared them, in respect they were pressed into the fleet against their wills, and did dispose them into several English men's hands upon good assurance that they should be forthcoming at all times. . . . But the Lord Deputy Fitzwylliam, having further advertisements from the north of the state of things in those parts, took occasion to make a journey thither and make his way through this province [Connacht], and in his passing along caused both these two Spaniards, which my brother had, to be executed, and the Dutch men and boys who had before been spared by me, reserving none but Don Lewes de Cordova and his nephew, whom I have here [at Athlone]. (C.S.P.I., p. 77.)

6.   Streedagh strand.

7.   de Cuellar gives no title to M'Glannagh as he does to O'Rourke, and O'Cahan later. The castle is Rossclogher (*stone fort on a promontory*). It stands on a small island which may once have been the "promontory".

8. Lough Melvin, which abounds in trout, salmon and gilaroo, is seven-and-a-half miles long and one-and-a-half miles wide. The river Drowse runs into the sea about two-and-a-half miles west of the lake close to Bundoran, which the English then called Bundrowse. The "town" which de Cuellar mentions may have been Kinlough (the head of the Lough) a little over a mile distant from the castle at the lake's western end.

9. These footpaths, or hidden causeways, were skilfully made after the fashion of those that earlier led to crannogs. The surface of the footpath lay beneath the water and followed a tortuous course so that only those who had made it, or who lived in the water-castle, could use it with impunity. Thus the dwellers were safeguarded from both wild animals and human marauders, whether rival chieftains or English desperados. There are remains of many island castles in Ireland where broken harps, brooches, combs, chased swords and scabbards, beads of amber, jet and glass set with enamel, and richly ornamented horse-trappings tell of a cultured people who had favoured lake habitations from the early Christian centuries or even earlier.

10. In what mixed language was this intricate conversation held? Gaelic is a subtle and difficult language in which de Cuellar would certainly not have been proficient. M'Glannagh knew some Latin from the Mass but probably no Spanish. No interpreters are mentioned and sign-language would not have been sufficient in this decisive agreement and preparation for a siege.

As late as 1845 Lord George Hill remarked about dwellers near the Bloody Foreland in Donegal, north of Lough Melvin:

> It often happens that a man has three dwellings—one in the mountains, another upon the shore, *and the third upon an island*, he and his family flitting from one to another of these habitations, as the various and peculiar herbage of each is thought to be beneficial to the cattle, which are supposed . . . to have a disease requiring a change of pasture, whilst in reality they only want more food. (*Facts from Gweedore*, Dublin, 1845.)

As we have seen, M'Glannagh had three such dwellings mentioned by de Cuellar, his "town" on the shore, Rossclogher in the lake, and his "booley" or milking-place on the heights of the hills where he took refuge from the Lord Deputy. Of the last Allingham says:

On the summit of a hill . . . is a circular enclosure about 220 feet in circumference; it is composed of earth, faced with stone work.

and he describes a mountain pathway leading to this "cattle-booley", "paved with stones enclosed by a kerb" (A/C., p. 17).

Booleying, or the folding and milking of cattle in upland pastures in the summer, was a custom of agricultural life maintained by the Irish until twenty years ago, accompanied by forgotten ritual festivities and ceremonies. Mountain grazing was often held on a system of joint tenure known as the rundale system, the origins of which are obscure, or a chieftain had his own grazing lands. Booleying, or seasonal nomadism, has had its influence on the Irish tendency to work hard in the spring and autumn only. The crops having been sown and the cattle taken to pasture in the hills as in Switzerland, Norway and Spain, the summer hill-dwelling places were inhabited until the harvest was gathered in the small fields below. Thus there might be found little clots of contented people—scattered mountain masses in all parts of the Island, especially where the coastal mountain ranges reared their craggy heads. But M'Glannagh drove his cattle before him in the unseasonable late autumn of 1588 for defensive, not pastoral, reasons. From his fastness above he could look down on the siege of Captain de Cuellar and his handful of men in the island castle, and on the nearby mainland church he had built. Today this is a roofless, aisleless ruin like the Abbey of Staad, with only east and west walls standing. At the northern end there is an obvious defensive slot cut in the masonry, now blocked up from within. Perhaps the Lord Deputy, foiled in gaining the castle, housed his men in the church and fortified it in this simple way.

The loophole would have served to mark down any man who trespassed that way.

To the north of Rossclogher Abbey, facing mountainwards, are the remains of what must once have been a burying-ground of the M'Glannagh's and their retainers, a scene of desolation, the fallen stones of the Abbey walls littering the ground. The side adjacent to a cart-track is made up of large stones—one of which bears a rough kind of cross-head, now lichened over. Between them sycamore seedlings have taken root and grown until they are large trees. By the lane's side there is what appears to be a primitive font or large Holy Water stoup, used in one of the field-walls as a convenient base stone, the pale-blue wild scabious blooming freely around it.

arquebuses and other arms. The chieftain embraced us and retired into the mountains, whither his people had already gone, and soon word spread through the country that Manglana's castle was preparing to resist and would not yield to the enemy, because a Spanish captain and other Spaniards were in it, and were defending it.(1)

The whole country applauded our courage, and the enemy were much enraged and advanced against the castle in full force, numbering about eighteen hundred men; they halted a mile and a half away, being unable to come closer because of the water that lay between, and from this position they tried to terrify us by hanging Spaniards and committing other outrages. Their trumpeter called on us repeatedly to leave the castle and they would spare our lives and give us free passage back to Spain. We told him to come closer to the tower as we could not understand him, showing him all the time that we made light of his threatening speeches.

For seventeen days they besieged us, after which our Lord was pleased to help us and deliver us from the enemy by sending dreadful storms and heavy falls of snow, such that the Lord Deputy was forced to raise the siege and return with all his men to Dublin, where he had his base and garrison. From thence he sent us messages warning us to keep out of his reach, and saying that in his own good time he would return to that part of the country.(2) We gave him an answer after our own hearts, and satisfactory also to the owner of the castle, who returned to his town and castle much relieved in mind as soon as he heard that the English had withdrawn.

He made much of us, declaring that we had proved ourselves most trusty friends; he put everything belonging to him at our disposal, and the chief men of the region did likewise. To me he offered one of his sisters in marriage; I thanked him gratefully but told him I would be content with a guide to take me to a place where I could embark for Scotland. He was unwilling to give me or any of the Spaniards who were with him leave to go, saying that the roads were not safe, but his sole purpose was to keep us there to defend him. So much friendship was not to my liking, and I therefore came to a secret agreement with four soldiers among my companions to depart one morning two hours before dawn so that they should not come after us; moreover one of Manglana's sons had told me the day before that his father had declared that I must not be allowed to leave his castle until the King of Spain sent soldiers to his country, and that he would put me in prison so that I could not get away. As a result of this information I dressed myself as best I could and set out with the four soldiers on the tenth morning after Christmas-day, of the year '88.(3)

I travelled through the mountains and uninhabited regions, suffering great hardships as God knows, and after twenty days' journey I reached the place where Alonso de Leyva, the Conde de Paredes and Don Tomas de Granvela (4) had perished, together with many other gentlemen whose names would fill a quire of paper. I went among the huts of some savages that were there, and learned from them about the terrible sufferings of our people who were drowned there, and was shown many jewels and valuables belonging to them.(5) This caused me much sorrow, and my distress was even greater when I found there was no ship to take me to the kingdom of Scotland; however one day they

*brought me news of a territory belonging to a native chief called
Prince Ocán,(6) where there were some boats about to embark for
Scotland.*

*I dragged myself thither, though I could scarcely move because
of the wound in one of my legs. As my life depended on it I
exerted all my strength in walking, but for all my haste the
boats had already been gone two days when I arrived. This
was no small grief to me, for I was in a miserable region full of
enemies, there being many English stationed in this port who
came every day to visit Ocán. I was suffering such great pain in
my leg at this time that I was quite unable to stand upon it; and
I was warned to be on my guard against the English, who would
do me an injury if they caught me, just as they had to other
Spaniards, and especially if they discovered who I was. I knew
not what to do, for the soldiers who had come with me had already
left me and gone to another and more distant port to look for a
ship. Seeing me alone and ill, some women had pity on me and
took me to their huts in the mountains, where they kept me in
safety for more than a month and a half, and tended my wound
so that it healed up and I felt well enough to go to Ocán's
village and speak with him. But he would neither hear nor see
me, for it was said that he had given his word to the Queen's
Lord Deputy not to let any Spaniard stay in his territory or even
pass through it.(7)*

*It happened that at this time the English who were quartered
in the place had gone to invade and take by force a neighbouring
territory, and that the Ocán and all his fighting men were with
them, so that it was possible to go freely about the village, which
was built of huts thatched with straw. Some exceedingly beautiful
girls were living there, with whom I became very friendly, and I
went to their houses now and again for conversation and company; but one evening when I was there two young Englishmen
came in, one of whom was a sergeant who knew me by name
but had never seen me, and after sitting down they asked me
whether I was a Spaniard and what I was doing there. I told
them I was, and that I was one of Don Alonso de Luçon's(8) men*

1. The castle of Rossclogher looks even more ruinous today than when Spotswood-Green photographed it in 1905–6. Time and weather do their insidious work. Allingham states that it was built "anterior to the reign of Henry VIII..."

> a peculiar structure, being built on an artificial foundation, somewhat similar to the "Hag's Castle" in Lough Mask, [in Co. Mayo] and to Cloughoughter Castle in the neighbouring county of Cavan....
>
> Rossclogher Castle is built on a foundation of heavy stones laid in the bed of the lake, and filled in with smaller stones and earth to above water-level. The substructure was circular in form ... encompassed by a thick wall probably never more than five feet in height. The walls of the castle are very thick, composed of freestone obtained from an adjacent quarry on the mainland. They are cemented together with the usual grouting of lime and coarse gravel, so generally used by the builders of old; the outside walls were coated with rough-cast, a feature not generally seen in old structures in the locality. Facing the south shore, which is about one hundred yards distant, are the remains of a bastion pierced for mus-ketry. The water between the castle and the shore is deep, and goes down sheer from the foundation. (A/C., pp. 16–17.)

I set out to find Rossclogher on a fine September autumn morning suffused with soft light, heading for the village of Kinlough at the western end of Lough Melvin. Close to the fine-gravelled road lined with ash trees there is a derelict estate, formerly owned by an Englishman, with high garden walls and old orchards, park-like trees and bent iron gates. The road runs under the Dartraigh mountains, with Truskmore rising to a height of over 2,000 feet.

By now it was raining softly. There were many white houses, some perched high up on the mountain's side, and high roadside hedges of the West Indian fuschia, with "their little red drops". In some of the gardens tall white gladioli, bent with rain and September winds, lay flattened on the ground.

The side-lane to Rossclogher with its twin wheel-tracks was

marked with donkeys' and horses' hooves in the middle grass
ridge. The deep ditches at the side were filled with meadow-
sweet and lined with wind-bitten sallies. There was a touch of
moorland round the bend, large blocks of stone lying about. A
solitary thatched cabin came into sight with turf-smoke coming
from the stubby chimney. On that side facing the road the
building had no windows, only a brown varnished door firmly
closed. No one was visible.

Passing through two gates of home-made construction, tied to
their posts with string, I reached a third with a pair of bicycles
leaning against it, those of two men approaching, one young
with an inquisitive sheepdog, the other old, toothless and half-
shaven, but full of courtesy. He would act as my guide and put
me on my way to the castle. Setting his scythe down carefully he
drew my attention to the profusion of wild berries that year, the
hollies towering fifteen feet above us and the orange-pink rose
hips interwoven amongst them. We had entered a small wood
thick with sallies, rowans, and small ash trees over which the
wild roses climbed possessively. At this point we passed a sur-
prisingly well-built barn with cut squared stones and Flemish
crow's-foot gables—stones probably taken from the abbey or cell
I also wanted to see.

"Go on-away easht through that meadow there, and ye'll see
the island with the Castle on it."

"And the abbey?" I asked.

"It's under ye," he replied succinctly, meaning that when I got
to the far pasture, it would be at a lower level beneath me.

I asked him what had become of the M'Glannagh's, whether
there were any hereabouts?

"There's neither fin nor feather of them left," and he concluded with an apocryphal tale of the last scion, a daughter,
"whom the fox was afther. And they moored her up in a cashel,
see?" Upon this he left me.

Turning back to look at castle and church I made out an
exceptionally level hayfield full of "bents", with a solitary mow
standing in it, where the old man with his scythe and the young

man with his dog had been mowing before I met them. So peaceful and silent was the scene in its cloud-mottled light that it was hard to envisage Fitzwylliam's siege—the shots and shouting, interspersed with the English trumpeter's code-commands, "Surrender and be pardoned", "Surrender or die".

The field through which I must pass to get to the shore was filled with thick, wet grass about a foot high, laid flat with wind and rain. Behind, flat-topped Glenavon mountain towered darkly above, its colour changing from grey to royal purple. I stumbled down over two broken field-walls passing several exceptionally fine thorn trees, buttressed by hollies. Before me Lough Melvin stretched pale blue and faintly ruffled.

Suddenly Rossclogher came in sight. It stands on an invisible island with reeds that dip to a fine point to the west. Although the level of the lake water was not high after a dry summer, there was sufficient depth of water round the ruin to enable one to visualize de Cuellar easily holding out against the Lord Deputy unless his men wished to risk drowning, or to be killed by well-aimed stone cannon balls, or shots from an arquebus. Today ivy clothes the crumbling mass of circular stone, so that even the loop-hole windows are hard to find and the birds nest in its swathes.

2. Fitzwylliam did not return and no mention of the siege of Rossclogher is given in the *State Papers*. Either Fitzwylliam was discomfited or thought this defeat a petty one, incommensurate in scale to the whole campaign in the west and north: de Cuellar's account is therefore of unique historic importance.

3. It is not clear what route de Cuellar took to reach the coast of Antrim. "Twenty days journey" does not tell us much. Allingham believes that he took the coast road, "the circuitous route round the coast of Donegal to Derry, and from thence to Dunluce". But this would seem an unnecessary hardship, and it is quite possible that, considering the lameness from which he suffered, his enforced periods of hiding, the bitter time of wet and cold, and his ignorance of the country, that de Cuellar could take as long as three weeks to travel inland over the mountains

towards Strabane, thence to Derry, across the Foyle, and thence through Limavady and Coleraine to some spot near the Giant's Causeway.

4. The Count de Paredes was the third in command of the Armada, excluding the General, the Duke of Medina Sidonia. The first of the Commanders was the Prince d'Ascoli, bastard son of Philip (C.S.P.S., p. 306). In the *Examination* of an Irish sailor, Machary of the Cross, Parades is set down by the English as "Count de Paris, or Perez?", and Don Tomas as de "gran Bello", a man much favoured with the King, of great revenue, and a natural Spaniard born" (C.S.P.I., pp. 98–9).

5. de Cuellar is here speaking of the loss of the last Armada ship recorded by name—*La Gerona*, a galleass which went down west of the Giant's Causeway. She was wrecked on "the rock of Bunboyes" near the mouth of the Bush river, hard by Ballintrae. It used to be said that the small bay named Port na Spaniagh, east of the Causeway, marked the site of the wreck. The Lord Deputy, anxious to raise the *Gerona*'s cannon for Her Majesty—he wrongly calls her a *galley*—speaks of the ship as departing from Killybegs towards the "Out Isles of Scotland for aid, was wrecked and many drowned off Bunboys near Dunluce" (C.S.P.I., pp. 62–3 and Spotswood-Green, pp. 441–2). Fitzwylliam wrote on October 27th/November 6th, but she was sunk on the 18th/28th of the month according to the evidence of an English naval captain, Nicholas Merryman, who states that 260 bodies were washed up "with certain wine"; and Captain George Thornton made a declaration, dated December 31st (O.S.), that

> as he passed the Rathlins and Skirrys (Skerries) . . . it was constantly affirmed by a gunner saved out of the galleas (sic) . . . that Don Alonso de Leyva was drowned. (C.S.P.I., pp. 68 and 99.)

The *Gerona* was one of the galleasses of Naples under Don Hugo de Moncada, a ship with 50 guns and when she set out from Lisbon with a complement of 169 soldiers and 120 sailors (C.S.P.S., p. 283). But by the time that she was cast away near Dunluce she was swollen with the men of two other wrecked ships and carried, according to the Pilot General of the Armada, Marolin de Juan, 1,300 men of whom only *nine* were saved (C.S.P.S., p. 500). (Don Alonso de Leyva had twice been shipwrecked before, in the *Rata Encoronada* and the *Duquesa Santa Ana.*)

The Spaniards from the *Gerona* were taken up and succoured by Sorley Boy MacDonnell, Lord of Dunluce and joint lord of the route to Scotland. Dunluce, a Viking stronghold perched on the craggy crest of an impregnable rock, exhibits today a *graffito* of a Viking galley from the early Christian centuries scratched on a carefully preserved stone built into the gatehouse wall, and other Viking relics found in a *souterrain*. The massive rock on which the Castle stands is penetrated by a natural tunnel beneath it, making escape and entrance to those who knew the treacherous tides hazardous but possible. Fought over again and again by Vikings and Anglo-Normans, by native clans and Scots invaders —MacQuillans, O'Donnells, MacDonnells ("freebooter immigrants from the Scottish Isles"), chief amongst them Sorley Boy: wrested from one clan by another, only to revert to the first once more; besieged and taken by the Lord Deputy, Sir John Perrott, in 1584 but, the minute his back was turned and he was safely in Dublin, re-seized by Sorley Boy—such is Dunluce's history.

This Gaelic chieftain, who proudly signs himself in a letter to O'Neill whose daughter he had wed *I am Somairle Bwee*, held the "strong castle", or the "castle of the sirens" during Armada year. It remained in the hands of his descendants until its recent transfer to the Government who preserve it as an ancient monument. Like the other powerful chieftains of the north his territory lay virtually outside English government rule, and together with them he was instrumental in sending some of the wrecked Spaniards across to Scotland. He did so as late as February 1588-9 (before de Cuellar reached the site of the *Gerona*'s wreck close-by), and after he had been "subjugated" by the English— that is had made his submission, throwing down his sword before Her Majesty's picture in Dublin Castle, "kissing the pantofle (slipper) of the same", and giving up one of his sons as a pledge (C.S.P.I., p. 85).

Thereafter, although pity moved him to aid the shipwrecked Spaniards he seems to have remained loyal to Elizabeth and James, who belatedly made his son first Earl of Antrim. On one occasion, in 1589, he invoked English aid against the Scots who, under a M'Lane or MacLean, threatened to come "with a great company of Irish gallies" against the north, causing Fitzwylliam to pray "her Majesty might write to the King of Scots to stay these kind of people". He appealed, too, to O'Neill, informing him that the Scots were embarking for Lough Foyle and begging him to "send to the Lord Deputy for shipping to be sent against them" (C.S.P.I., pp. 226-7). Yet, such was the confusion in a still disunited Ireland that only two months earlier Sir Brian O'Rourke had pleaded with Sorley Boy to send contingents of Scots to aid him in Breffni, or at least this is what Byngham, reporting to the Lord Deputy, believed on hearsay.

6. This was the head of the sept of O'Cahan (spelt by the English variously as O'Chane, O'Cane, O'Cahane and O'Kane, but pronounced with a broad *a* in Gaelic, so that de Cuellar's phonetic approximation is once more correct). The Lordship of O'Cahan of Derry had been established before 1300. In writing to Edward I the chief of the sept signed himself *King of Keinaght* (Connaght). de Cuellar's O'Cahan was a cousin of the great O'Neill, Earl of Tyrone, whose territory lay east and south of Lough Foyle including the important town of Derry. In 1592, in an eleven-page declaration made by the Archbishop of Cashel, he is listed as first in importance under O'Neill (C.S.P.I., pp. 489-500). O'Cahan had

> by custom power to name and confirm out of the principal house, O'Neill, when O'Neill is dead, in such sort that if any will take upon him to be O'Neill, being not named or chosen by O'Cahan, he is not to be obeyed nor taken for O'Neill. If any should undertake the name of O'Neill, not appointed by O'Cahan, the people will think themselves not bound in conscience to obey him. This O'Cahan's country,

lying by the sea side, may easily be won from him upon the prince's misliking. (C.S.P.I., p. 345.)

Here is an example of tanistry in effect, and it perfectly explains M'Glannagh's attachment to Sir Brian O'Rourke, his stubborn loyalty to him and his belief that he owed allegiance and support to O'Rourke rather than to the English Sovereign, or Crown.

In 1590 Sir John Perrot advised that the great Earl of Tyrone (O'Neill) who had been brought up by Sir Henry Sydney and in the Palace of the Earl of Leicester in London, and who frequented the court of Elizabeth, should be compelled to renounce all claim to "O'Cahan's country" for the better ordering of the province of Ulster.

In this country the O'Cahans had four castles. The earliest appears to have been built at a place above the river Roe, about two miles south of Limavady (*the Leap of the Dog*), in what is now County Derry. This picturesque name derives from a legend that when the chief of the O'Cahans was once in distress his wolfhound leapt across the river bearing in his collar a message announcing relief from the Dungiven branch of the family. Dungiven was their second stronghold, near the meeting place of three rivers: its bawn, huge and bare, remains to remind us of the former power of this northerly sept. The last of the Dungiven branch was imprisoned in the Tower of London for eight years where he languished until he died, without a trial, his confiscated lands later being granted by James I to one of the London City Companies.

The third castle, east of the Giant's Causeway at Dunseverick on the coast, was built on the foundations of a rock-fortress mentioned in the early *Triads* as one of the three great buildings of ancient Ireland, and in the legends of the Red Branch Knights as housing one of the legendary heroes famed for his exploits. A fourth castle of the O'Cahans stood above the salmon-filled river Bann at Castleroe, south of Coleraine (*the Ferny Corner*).

When we come to de Cuellar's mention of O'Cahan's "territory", to which he was directed after passing close to the place where the *Gerona* had been wrecked (Portballintrae), we have to determine which of the O'Cahan "castles, towns, and ports" he is speaking of. At first this would seem to be Dunseverick. But after careful consideration of what de Cuellar tells us of his sub-sequent flight from O'Cahan's village and castle, putting this *behind* him, and of another Irish castle and place of refuge before he embarked for Scotland, it seems that *Castleroe* is the O'Cahan castle indicated, and *Coleraine* the port. The fact that Coleraine is now known chiefly as a plantation town, whose prosperity dates from the time of James I, has obscured the knowledge of its great antiquity. A mile south of the town there stands a huge mound, the royal palace of a ruler of the first century, used about 1200 for the site of a new castle by John de Courcy. In the fifth century it was linked with St. Patrick and—seven hundred years later—St. Bernard of Clairvaux refers to it as "a city". What is more relevant for us is that Coleraine was formerly a *port*, at the head of the navigable reach of the river Bann, only superseded in size and importance by Derry in the sixteenth century. Pro-fessor O'Reilly concurs in the opinion that the castle mentioned by de Cuellar stood near Coleraine, or between it and Lough Foyle.

7.   The change in heart of O'Cahan towards the Spaniards seems to be linked with that of King James, at the time of O'Rourke's flight to Scotland. The English were increasing their surveillance and measures of restriction, their tortures, hangings and "put-tings to the sword". The north and far west of Ireland, which had remained outside their control, were now being brought under it with greater severity. In a few years Derry would be subdued and taken (1600) and the Flight of the Earls, O'Donnell and O'Neill, was imminent (1607). O'Cahan, with a blood relation in the Tower, probably went in fear of his life.

That O'Cahan had earlier been protective and sympathetic to the Spaniards we know from the long *Statement* of two Spanish servants, quoted from later, in which they recount their adven-tures after the wreck of *La Trinidad Valencera*, three months before de Cuellar reached O'Cahan's country. These men were directed to Cornelius, Bishop of Down and Connor (*not* of

Killaloe as Hume suggested, see C.S.P.I., p. 63), whom the Lord
Deputy called "this obstinate enemy of God" and recommended
making an end of him. He assisted some of the survivors to reach
Scotland: others who were wounded:

> were sent under a guide to the house of a savage gentleman,
> O'Cahan, where they remained three days, both he and his
> people displaying great sympathy with them in their suffer-
> ings, feeding them and waiting on them hand and foot. On
> the fourth day they went with another guide to a brother
> of his, also named O'Cahan, twelve miles from here
> [O'Dogherty's Castle, the editor presumes]. He also wel-
> comed us with the same kindness as his brother had done.
> The day after our arrival mass was said for us but this was an
> exception in our honour, as they usually have mass only
> once a week. On the third day after their arrival he sent
> them with another guide and letters to another gentleman
> named Sorley Boy [O'Donnell] begging him to provide
> them with a boat, as they were Catholics as he was; this
> gentleman possessing vessels as he lives on an arm of the sea.
> [Sorley Boy was Lord of Dunluce Castle, near which the
> *Gerona* had been wrecked, and joint lord of the route]. He
> received them with much kindness and kept them twenty
> days, mass being said for them. There were at the time no
> boats there, but he sent for some three miles off. Two boats
> were sent and eighty soldiers embarked in them, to be taken
> to an island off Scotland, which is only 10 miles off, the rest
> remaining in the castle until the boats should return.

(Sorley Boy was either at his castle of Dunseverick, or Dunaney,
less than a mile west of Ballycastle, where he died in 1590.)

Corroboration of the increasing severity towards the Spaniards
north of Ireland is given in the next paragraph.

> In the meanwhile the Governor in Dublin [Fitzwylliam] had
> learned that this gentleman [Sorley Boy] had sheltered the
> Spaniards, and sent to tell him in the Queen's name not to
> ship any more Spaniards on pain of death, and confiscation
> of all his property, and to surrender to the English those he
> still had with him.

Irish Tourist Board

DUNLUCE CASTLE, CO. ANTRIM

Irish Tourist Board

The Blaskets from Slea Head, Co. Kerry

The Irish chieftain made a spirited reply—"he would rather lose his life and goods and those of his wife and children than barter Christian blood".

"He had," he said, "dedicated his sword to the defence of the Catholic faith and those who held it, and in spite of the Governor, the Queen, and all England, he would aid and embark the rest of the Spaniards who came to him; and he came back to them [the Spaniards] with tears in his eyes, and told them the Governor's demand and his reply thereto. *So when the boats came back he shipped the rest.*" (C.S.P.S., pp. 507–8. Italics mine.)

8.   This was obviously a feint to save his life for de Cuellar had never been with Don Alonso de Luçon, either on his ship or in his company. It is interesting to see how the Spaniards and Irish, cut off from orthodox channels of information, kept themselves abreast of events by word of mouth.

Don Alonso, Colonel of the Regiment of Naples and one of the six Maestres de Campo, each of whom commanded a company in addition to having general control of his regiment, had been in the thick of the battle in the Narrow Seas on August 2nd with his ship, the *Trinidad Valencera*. This large merchantman had remained with the broken Armada round the Scottish coasts, but springing a serious leak in a gale on September 12th she was forced to anchor in Glenagivney or Glanganvey Bay, today called Kinegoe, or Kinnagoe, on the Ordnance Maps. This lies west of Lough Foyle and Inishowen Head. About 600 of her men, together with those of the 'Barque of Hamburg' who had gone down so suddenly in the North Sea that all her stores were lost, landed on this northerly Irish shore. The Spaniards found themselves in the country of O'Dougherty of Inishowen, a mountainous land still remote and largely unknown.

On the 14th/24th of the month the brothers Hovenden, or Ovington, ardent in the Queen's service, reported having attacked and made the men prisoners, including an officer who had commanded as many as 30,000 men. Although the figure is exaggerated tenfold this indicates Don Alonso de Luçon. Informed

I

by O'Dougherty they had earlier, on the 8th/18th, reported the "drowning" of the *Valencera* together with 2–3,000 men to the Lord Deputy from "Castle Berte", and on the same day enquired of Tyrone what he intended to do with the men who had landed. The Hovendens were foster-brothers and henchmen of the great O'Neill, "commanding Irish companies in English pay", and it is said that Henry was "the secretary and trusted adviser of Tyrone". We do not know what Tyrone replied to the brothers' appeal for information as to what he would do. It seems unlikely that he would have authorized the treacherous part the Hovendens took in butchering those Spaniards who laid down their arms and gave themselves up in the belief that they would be honourably treated. The brothers had, of course, the examples of Lord Grey and of Raleigh for the annihilation of the Italians and Spaniards at Smerwick in 1580, and of the O'Malleys of Clare Island in Armada-year. But the Hovendens or Ovingtons, more English than Irish by name and possibly by ancestry, have been called Irish, and against them has been laid the heavy reproach of being the sole example (bar two) of Irishmen who "slaughtered the shipwrecked Spaniards in large numbers". In his Examination at Drogheda in October Don Alonso de Luçon expressly states that the Irish "savages" slew none of their company before they yielded to the Hovendens' lieutenant. On the contrary, although they took gold and a cloak "laid with gold lace" they brought them garrons and butter which they sold to the starving men (Laughton II, pp. 271–6).

The bay in which the *Valencera* was wrecked is smaller than Port Ballintrae where the *Gerona* foundered. Today it is more beautiful since it has not been built over, and because the rocks here are a limestone grey.

I was in O'Dogherty's country at the time of year when the ship sank. The hills here dip and rise like round-headed waves. The field patterns—rough squares and oblongs of yellow, green and brown (still-standing oats, pasture, and rough leys in which gorse and heath are taking over from cultivated land now reverting to its ancient state)—were of course not there in Armada days. But it is likely that some oats were grown for man and beast even in 1588, and the hand-bound sheaves of today, standing together in leaning stooks, orange-gold against the blue sea, are a timeless feature. The old woman dressed in black, quietly driving her cattle, and the old man venturing forth into the soft rain with no overcoat to fetch turf from the stack for his smoking fire, except for their modern clothing are timeless too; and the horses, except that they are larger than the Irish *gearrans* of the sixteenth century, standing with their tails to the wind against a rough-piled stone wall, might have been there when the surviving Spaniards came dripping and cold ashore.

The place where the English attacked with only 150 men was at Illagh, "Sir John O'Dogherty's town", whither the ship-wrecked and starving Spaniards had marched and sought refuge, about eighteen miles inland (C.S.P.I., p. 42).

Although Sir John, unlike O'Cahan, had officially gone over to the English he seems, like many Irish princes to have been confused between his native loyalties in conflict with what reason told him was wise for their safety. He parleyed with the Spaniards and received a placatory gift of arms, but more suspect, he actually aided the Spaniards out of Christian humanity. More men would have been drowned

> if not that O'Dogherty's men went unto them with boats and did bring them to the shore, and withal part of O'Dogherty's men have been familiar among the Spaniards since their landing, and it is said that O'Dogherty himself has been in speeches [sic] with them, which I think the rather to be true, for that he hath a fair target [a round shield or buckler], a murrion [a kind of helmet without a visor], and a halberd of theirs, which argueth to be received rather as a gift, than to be had by any other means. (C.S.P.I., p. 36.)

O'Dogherty had earlier been in touch with Fitzwylliam on his journey through the north to haggle over sureties for beeves for her Majesty, and over (human) pledges. He was later to be dramatically rescued from Dublin Castle through the bribe of hogsheads of salmon sent to the Lord Chancellor's cellar, "and

that, too, without the poor constable getting his fees", an incident
which has a Falstaffian ring (C.S.P.I., p. 500).

When the assessment of the lands of the northern princes was
made by the Archbishop of Cashel for Her Majesty, in 1592, it
was stated that O'Dogherty with four other chieftains was
"under the exaction of O'Donnell", and every five of these men
"have their castles and land by the sea side" (C.S.P.I., p. 309).
His castle at Illagh, Aillagh, or Ellogh, with its tragic and un-
savoury memories, is difficult to find since the castle is a crumbled
ruin and his "town" vanished. If, as Spotswood-Green asserts, it
"lies to the north of the railway line between Londonderry and
Buncrana" the Ordnance Maps now spell it Galliagh, perhaps the
name's original form.

Here Don Alonso de Luçon, Ponce de Leon, and other renowned officers found the English in league with O'Dogherty
and in occupation of his castle. But, like de Cuellar, they were
directed to a good Bishop, also in a castle, for succour.
O'Dogherty seems thus, like O'Cahan, to have been sheltering
an ecclesiastic who helped the Spaniards while he, as head of
his sept, gave outward allegiance to the English Queen.

The account of de Luçon's adventures told in the longest and
most graphic detail comes from the Spanish servants Juan de
Nova and Francisco de Borja, one of whom had been in Don
Alonso's company. The journey from the coast—where they
first marched along the rocks—to the castle, about eighteen miles
inland, took the Spaniards four days. Don Alonso sent word to
the Bishop (of Down and Connor) begging him to advise them.
He told them to approach the castle and to fire their arquebusses
so as to make an appearance of taking it by force to prevent the
Queen's officers from saying that he (O'Dogherty) had surrendered it voluntarily, "and it would then be surrendered to
them". The Spaniards went forward and arrived within sight of
the castle, "when those within discharged a piece of artillery
towards the part where the Queen's garrison was". Don Alonso
became suspicious and retreated to another dismantled castle
hardby, near a marsh. At that they discovered the English garrison

approaching them. The opposing men halted: drums were beaten and a parley ensued. The English enquired what the Spaniards were doing in the Queen's territories. The Spaniards replied that they had been shipwrecked and asked only for another ship to convey them home. They were informed that this was impossible and that they must surrender. The Spaniards replied that they would rather die fighting like proper Spaniards. The English then threatened that 3,000 men would come shortly (a reference to Fitzwylliam's entreated force), and that all their throats would then be cut. Don Alonso still refused to surrender. They halted throughout the night, and were attacked on the following day, the skirmish continuing throughout the second night. The next morning the drums sounded for another parley. The Spanish officers went "down to the bog" to discuss matters. The English advised the Spaniards that it would be best for them to surrender and be sent to Dublin where there were many prisoners of note. Many promises were made by the 'English' major, an affected Irishman by the name of Kelly. Cut off from all supplies and dying of hunger, Don Alonso agreed to surrender "on fair terms of war", and provided that the English kept their promise to allow each man to retain his best suit of clothes. The English agreed and the Spaniards laid down their arms. Upon getting them to the "other side of the bog" the English fell upon the men "in a body", despoiling them of all that they had, leaving them naked and killing anyone who resisted. Don Alonso, taken prisoner, complained. The English officer replied that the killings were not by his orders and gave his word, such as it was, that the captive Spaniards would be re-clothed when they reached yet another castle two miles off where he intended to spend the night. The road proved too rough even for 'Major' Kelly and he gave orders to bivouac in the open for the night. The English formed a square inside which they placed Don Alonso and the other prisoners, including one or two gentlemen volunteers, many of whom were attached to the Armada, two attachés, several Captains, the Chaplain General and Judge of the regiment, the Vicar of the shoeless Carmelites of Lisbon, and two other friars. The soldiers were "left a stone's-throw away, naked, in which manner they passed the night". At daybreak the massacre began. The English came to

> separate some other officers who were amongst the soldiers, and put them inside the square with the rest. The remaining soldiers were then made to go into an open field, and a line of the enemy's [the English] harquebussiers approached them on one side and a body of his cavalry on the other, killing over 300 of them with lance and bullet; 150 Spaniards managed to escape across a bog, most of them wounded, and sought refuge in the castle of Duhort (O'Dogherty) where Bishop Cornelius received them and conveyed 100 or so, who were unwounded, to the Island of Hibernia [Hebrides or Scotland]. Those who were wounded remained in the castle, under the care of the people there, who were Catholics, but many of them died every day. (C.S.P.S., pp. 506–10.)

Juan de Nova and Francisco de Borja, eyewitnesses of the slaughter, were two of those who survived. Eventually thirty-two of the Spaniards reached Scotland, and finally Havre de Grace and Bordeaux. In Scotland

> they learnt from a savage who spoke Latin that, on the same day that the English had massacred the soldiers, they had conveyed the colonel Don Alonso de Luçon and the rest of the officers on foot, all naked as they were, to Dublin . . . where they were put into prison, except those who died on the road of hunger, thirst, and exhaustion. (C.S.P.S., pp. 506–10.)

Another important survivor of *La Trinidad Valencera* was her Master, who made his way to London via Scotland. He confirms what de Cuellar has told us of the treatment that he received from the Irish country-people—that they plundered the Spaniards, relieving them of jewels, arms and clothing but treated them well afterwards, "giving them food and lodging on the road" (C.S.P.S., p. 492). A third account by hearsay is given by Marolin de Juan, Pilot General of the Armada (C.S.P.S., p. 500).

Finally the *Spanish State Papers* give us details of how de Luçon and his aristocratic companions were haggled over for months, stretching into years. First they were marched to Drogheda Castle on the Boyne, grim stronghold of the Danish marauders and later of the Anglo-Normans of the Pale. Examined here on October 13th/23rd Don Alonso stated that he was

Master of the camp of the *tercia* of Naples, being 10 ensigns containing 1,800 men. (C.S.P.I., p. 58.)

(A *terzo* is a regiment of 3,000 men furnished by Italian states to the Kings of Spain: hence the misleading figure of 30,000 given by the Hovendens earlier as the number of men which a single man, taken prisoner, had commanded.)

A *List of Prisoners in the Town of Drogheda in Ireland* (1588) is headed by the name of "Don Alonso de Luçon, Colonel" followed by those of other officers, together with those of a doctor, a Greek sailor, a ship's clerk, a barber, some servants and three Italian drummers: "three who have died in the town", one of them a younger brother of Don Alonso's, one who died "crossing a river", four "very ill and not known whether dead or alive", and, most pitiful of all at the list's close—"Died before they surrendered, Don Pedro de Salto, aged from 14–15 years". So young and a soldier, perhaps one of the noble lads attached to the Armada for a "lark" (C.S.P.I., pp. 584–5 and 106).

More than a year after the sinking of the *Valencera*, in December 1589, the Spanish Ambassador at Paris is writing to Philip II about the exchange of Don Alonso and some of his companions. Towards Midsummer 1591, Don Alonso is in London to which he had been sent by the Lord Deputy in January 1588–9. He writes courteously and clearly to Burghley begging for a decision on this long delayed and dispiriting matter. The appeal is signed by him and Don Nino de Lasso, Don Luis de Cordoba and Don Gonzalo Fernandez de Cordoba, all of whom had survived the bloody Illagh slaughter, in Inishowen, nearly five years ago. The matter of ransom may have been purposefully delayed, but was complicated by the death of Secretary Walsyngham in the meantime. Don Alonso and his companions appear to have been living in the house of Sir Horatio Pallavicini but their letter is merely dated "21st of June, 1590, From this house" [London] (C.S.P.S., pp. 548, 563).

who had surrendered to them a few days earlier: that I had been unable to leave the region on account of the wound in my leg, but that I was at their service and ready to obey their commands. They told me I must wait a little, and then go with them to the city of Dublin where many important Spaniards were imprisoned. I told them I could not walk nor go with them, and they sent in search of a horse to carry me. I said that I would most willingly do what they asked and go with them, whereupon they were satisfied and began dallying with the girls. But their mother made signs to me to escape through the door, and this I did with all haste, leaping over ditches and making my way through dense thickets until the Ocán's castle was out of sight.

I followed this course until nightfall, when I came to a very large lake (1) on the shores of which I saw a herd of cows. I was approaching to see if there was anyone with them who would tell me where I was, when I observed two young savages coming to fetch their cows and drive them up the mountain where they and their parents had taken refuge out of terror of the English. I stayed with them there for two days and was treated with much kindness; then one of these lads had to go to the Prince of Ocán's village to find out what news or rumours were going about, and he saw the two Englishmen searching for me in a great rage, for they had now discovered who I was, and asking everyone they met if they had seen me. When he saw this, the lad had the good nature to return to his hut and tell me what was happening, so that I was obliged to leave very early in the morning and go in search of a bishop, who was living in retirement in a castle (2) seven leagues away, whither he had fled from the English. This bishop was a truly Christian man; he went about disguised as a savage, and I assure you that I could not restrain my tears when I approached to kiss his hand. He had twelve Spaniards staying with him until he could pass them over into Scotland, and he was much pleased at my arrival, and more so when the soldiers told him I was a captain.

During the six days I spent with him he treated me with all possible kindness, and he gave orders for a boat to be sent for, fully equipped to take us over to Scotland, a journey which usually takes two days. He gave us provisions for the voyage and said mass for us in the castle; he talked with me also of various matters relating to the loss of the kingdom and the help His Majesty had given them; he told me that he intended to come to Spain as soon as possible after landing us in Scotland, where he warned me to show great patience, because most of the inhabitants were Lutherans and there were few Catholics. This bishop was called Don Reimundo Termi, and he was bishop of Times,(3) an honourable and just man—may God watch over him and deliver him from his enemies.

That same day, just as it was growing light, I embarked in a wretched boat.(4) We were eighteen persons in all, and during the day a contrary wind arose and forced us to run before it at the mercy of God, in the direction of Shetland, which we reached at dawn the next day, with our boat almost water-logged and the mainsail torn. We went ashore and gave thanks to God for His mercies in bringing us here alive; and two days afterwards, the weather being favourable, we set sail for Scotland, where we arrived in three days, having been in great danger from the quantity of water shipped by our wretched boat. Blessed be God who delivered us from so many and such sore trials and brought us to a land where there was hope of safety.

It was said that the King of Scotland sheltered all the Spaniards who landed in his kingdom, giving them clothes and sending them by ship to Spain, but we found the contrary to be true: he was good to none of them, nor did he give away a single real out of charity, and all those of us who came to his kingdom suffered the greatest privations. We lived there for more than six months as naked as we had arrived from Ireland, as did those who came from other places in search of safety and a passage to Spain.

I am even of the opinion that he was prevailed upon by the Queen of England to hand us over to her, and had it not been for the help of some Catholic noblemen of that kingdom (5) (where there are many such, and great gentlemen) who spoke on our behalf to the King and at the Councils that were held on the subject, we should undoubtedly have been betrayed and handed over to the English.

The King of Scotland is of no account, nor has he the authority or dignity of a king, and he takes no step nor eats a single mouthful except by order of the Queen. This is the cause of great dissension among the nobility, who bear him no good-will, but wish to have done with him and see the King [Philip of Spain], our lord and master, in his place, so that he may set up God's church again which has fallen into such sad ruin in that country. This they told us many times over, almost in tears, declaring that they hoped by God's grace that day would come soon.(6)

As I have said, these noblemen maintained us all the time we were there, giving us money and showing us great kindness; they sorrowed over our misfortunes and begged us to have patience and bear with these people who called us idolaters and bad Christians, and uttered a thousand heresies to us. For if any-one should answer them back they would fall on him and kill him, and it was impossible to exist or remain in such a wicked country and with such a bad king★ . . . A message was sent to the Duke of Parma,★ . . . as a pious prince, His Highness (7) was greatly grieved at this, and did all he could to help us★ . . . to the King, so that he should allow us to go free from his country, and to the Catholics and our friends most grateful thanks on the part of His Majesty, together with very friendly letters.

There was a Scottish merchant living at this time in Flanders, who offered his services and arranged with His Highness to come to Scotland for us and ship us on four vessels with all necessary provisions and bring us to Flanders, His Highness paying five ducats (8) for every Spaniard conveyed to Flanders.

★ Torn and illegible.

The agreement was concluded and he came to fetch us, and embarked us unarmed and naked as he found us, and conveyed us by way of the ports of the Queen of England, which promised us safe conduct through all the fleets and ships of her kingdom. This was all treachery, for a treaty had been made with the ships of Holland and Zealand, by which it was agreed that they should put to sea and lie in wait for us off the bar of Dunkirk and put us all to the sword to the last man. The Dutch carried out this order and waited for us for a month-and-a-half at the said port of Dunkirk, and there they would have caught us all but for God's help. By God's grace, out of the four vessels in which we sailed two got away and ran ashore, where they went to pieces. Then the enemy, seeing our efforts to escape, put us under heavy artillery fire, so that we were obliged to throw ourselves into the sea, believing that our last moment had come. They could not send boats from the port of Dunkirk to help us because they were receiving a lively cannonade from the enemy; there were heavy seas and high winds also, so that we were in the utmost peril of all being lost. However we flung ourselves onto planks of wood, although some Scottish soldiers and a captain were drowned. I reached the shore wearing nothing but my shirt, and some of Medina's (?) soldiers who were there came to my help. It was a pitiful sight to see us enter the town, once more reduced to nakedness, while almost in front of our eyes the Dutch were cutting to pieces two hundred and seventy Spaniards arriving in the boat which had brought us to Dunkirk, and leaving no more than three alive. This deed they are now paying for, as more than four hundred Dutchmen taken prisoner since then have been beheaded. I desired to write to you concerning all these things.

From the city of Antwerp,(9) 4th October, 1589.

FRANCISCO DE CUELLAR.

1. Lough Foyle. Lough Swillymor (*the great lake of the shadows*) would be too far west, and there are no large loughs east or south of Anagh Castle, or Castle Roe.

2. Probably Annagh Castle, yet another fortress of the O'Cahans on the right bank of the Foyle close to Derry.

The castles of Anagh, Limavady, Coleraine and Castle Roe commanded the coastal route and behind it lay a line of retreat up the Roe Valley and through . . . other passes. Remote and difficult of access from Dublin . . . and within easy reach of Scotland, from which war supplies could be obtained, O'Cahan's country proved in the wars of Elizabeth's reign to be a strategic area of the first importance. . . . From the beginning of the Queen's reign Lord Deputies repeatedly led punitive expeditions into his territory but, lacking a base of operations, were as often compelled to retire with nothing accomplished save a trail of devastation. O'Cahan's territory was not finally reduced . . . till at the beginning of the 17th century, permanent military posts were established at Derry and Coleraine. (*The Londonderry Plantations*, T. W. Moody, Belfast, 1939, pp. 50–2, 56, 58.)

Prior to the seventeenth century it possessed a distinct identity. The O'Cahans did not cede Anagh and their land between the Foyle and the Fahan to the English forces, under Docwra, until after the Irish disaster at Kinsale (1601).

Or it might be the old castle at Derry (from Coleraine 31 miles). Having joined forces with O'Donnell against Shane O'Neill in October 1566, Lord Deputy Sir Henry Sydney penetrated to Derry, turned the ancient Abbey into a fortress and posted a strong garrison here. Their colonel was killed within a short time and two-thirds of the garrison perished of cold, disease, and fire caused by a spark from a smith's forge blowing up the powder magazine. In 1600 a more serious attempt was made by Sir Henry Docwra, who also fortified the Abbey. "Nothing so formidable had been seen in those parts previously". (See *Journal of Royal Society of Antiquaries of Ireland*, Vol. XLV Consecutive Series, Dublin, 1916, pp. 209 et seq.)

Docwra's Abbey-Castle would have been too late for de Cuellar's date, but it is probable that English forces made use of the previous fortifications whenever they attempted to garrison men in Derry or to campaign in the district.

3. This was the Bishop of Derry. It seems incredible that Allingham, an Anglo-Irishman and editor of de Cuellar's *Letter*, should not have troubled to identify this prelate who played the part of the Good Samaritan in the Spaniard's life. It looks as though the word *Termi*, printed in Duro's *La Armada Invencible*, is indecipherable in the original manuscript, or the error is either a scribe's or de Cuellar's own. No such place as *Times* exists in Ireland, and Tuam, which writers have fancifully substituted, is an incompatible area for the Bishop's activities. It is possible that de Cuellar wrote *Terri*. The Irish pronunciation of *d* and *t* is often almost identical and de Cuellar has once again set down what he heard phonetically. The identification is made possible by de Cuellar giving the Bishop of Derry's Christian name— *Reimundo*. This was *Redmund* (O'Gallagher), in Latin *Redmundus*. The two men must have conversed in Latin, which we have seen was the custom between educated men in Ireland at this time.

There are as many as six references to the Bishop of Derry in the *State Papers Ireland* between the years 1588–92. The first is in the letter of a certain Patrick Foxe who reports to Walsyngham (September 26th, 1588):

> that a great number of the Spaniards that were stript naked by the soldiers that serve under the leading of both the Hovendens, are now come to the other Spaniards that landed in M'Sweeny's country [Donegal], and thither brought by the Bishop of Derry, a most seditious papist, and a man very like to procure great aid to the Spaniards if he can . . . (C.S.P.I., p. 44.)

Next, Fitzwylliam forwards to Burghley a licence from

> Redmund, Bishop of Derry, to Cornelius, Bishop of Down & Connor [who had helped the survivors from the *Valencera*] granting the power of absolution, etc., for one year. Tamlar Church, July 1, 1588. (C.S.P.I., p. 63.)

From then onwards both bishops were marked men, and it was a case of "set a bishop to catch a bishop".

The next reference to the Bishop of Derry comes more than two years later, by which time de Cuellar had safely reached the continent. It was made in the hand of the apostatized Archbishop of Cashel, Myler MacGrath, whom we have met before encountering O'Rourke as he went to the gallows. The Archbishop had originally been nominated by the Pope to the bishopric of Down, but having gone over to the English and Protestantism he was nominated by the Crown to Cashel and Emly, to which he cunningly succeeded in adding Waterford and Lismore, plus 77 lesser benefices. At the instigation of Burghley and others he was at pains to draw up a list of "Popish bishops, doctors and seminary priests in Ireland" which Byngham duly forwarded to Elizabeth's chief minister:

> In Ulster there is one Redmond [sic] O'Gallaghor [sic], Bishop of Derry, Pope's legate, and custos of Armagh, one of three Irish bishops that were in the Council of Trent [the Council's last session was in 1562–3: the Bishop of the neighbouring diocese of Raphoe was the second of the three.] He rides from place to place with pomp and company, as was the custom in Queen Mary's days. The clergy there have even changed the time according to the Pope's new invention. [England was the last to adopt the Calendar proclaimed by Pope Gregory XIII in 1582 and used by most of western Europe by 1587.] He has been several times before the governors of that land [Italy] upon protection, and yet he is suffered to enjoy his bishoprick these twenty-six years past and more. (C.S.P.I., p. 375.)

Again, two years later, in September 1592, both the Lord Deputy and Chancellor Loftus are inveighing against the Bishop of Derry, whom they in turn roundly call "the traitor", and they enclose for Lord Burghley a faculty, or dispensation, for one William Nugent granted by the bishop, "to hold certain lands, possessions, and tithes pertaining to churches and monasteries". They also enclosed a complicated report as to how this faculty had fallen into the hands of the Bishop of Meath (Thomas Jones, a Welshman) who in his turn lashes the Bishop of Derry—

> that traitorous Rome-runner ... whose heart has been fraught with treason even from his cradle. (C.S.P.I., pp. 595–6.)

The name Derry, visual and descriptive like all Celtic place-names, means "an oak wood". Its history dates from the foundation by St. Columcille of a monastic house there in 546—his favourite cell which he affectionately calls

> ... my own oak grove,
> Little cell, my home, my love.

It became an ecclesiastical centre of great importance and, owing to its position on the Foyle near the sea-filled Lough of the same name, a settlement coveted and preyed on by successive marauders. From the ninth to the eleventh century it was recurrently ravaged by the Danes; its ancient Abbey, "the Black Church", was destroyed. Redmund's predecessor by 400 years, the first Bishop of Derry, an Abbot, built the Great Church or Cathedral, destroyed in the Siege of 1689. Here, Redmund, before his services were proscribed, celebrated the divine rites and mysteries. Derry was never occupied by the Anglo-Normans and remained unsubdued by the English until 1600. It is significant that a year later, in 1601, we find among the names of Irish martyrs (1534–1603) that of Redmund, Bishop of Derry, together with thirty-two Dominican monks from the Priory in Derry. The net had closed round him as English military power in the north was more perfectly established under Docwra. The Archbishop of Cashel had had his way.

Since writing the paragraph above on the Bishop of Derry I find that Professor O'Reilly also identified him in 1893. He suggests that de Cuellar, conversing in Latin, misunderstood the word *tenens* in Bishop Redmund's Latin title—Redmundus Derensis Episcopus ac Primatis locum *tenens*—or, if he bore a document in this language for transmission to Scotland or Spain, misread it: hence *Times*.

4. *charruas*, the word here used for an unknown type of boat is now obsolete. We know from the *State Papers Ireland* that the English called certain boats manned by oars, used in ferrying men back-and-forth from Ireland to Scotland, *Irish galleys*. It is probably these, a type with which de Cuellar, used to the larger Mediterranean galleys was unfamiliar, which are meant (see p. 29).

It would be interesting to know from which ports de Cuellar, and earlier the two Spanish servants and their 78 companions, sailed. Doubtless many small coves, hardly large enough to be dignified with the title of port, were used. De Cuellar stated that it generally took two days to reach Scotland, and the servants that Scotland "was only 10 miles off". The distance between the vicinity of Lough Foyle and Ayr is about 110 miles. But they were embarking from, and landed in, different places. Dunseverick (Antrim) was a recognized port but there are more sheltered bays to the west, between it and Lough Foyle. Small craft sometimes put out from Dunluce at which some of the Armada ships intended to fire believing it to be held by the English, but instead they mistook the rock-formations of the Giant's Causeway and fired at their 'chimneys'.

Derry in the late eighteenth and nineteenth centuries was the traditional port of embarkation for Glasgow and was annually used by the thousands of migratory harvesters employed in England crossing from the counties of Derry and Donegal. This traditional usage implies an older well-known and well-used route. It is probable that de Cuellar embarked on the Derry route rather than further east from Dunseverick, as Allingham asserts.

5. According to a list drawn up by Burghley in 1592 the most influential of these had been and were the Earls of Bothwell, Huntly, Crawford, Errol and Montrose; and the Lords, Seton, Livingstone, Maxwell, Herries, Sanquhar, Gray, Ogilvie, Fleming and Urquhart. To these might be added the Earls of Argyll and Angus, Lord Semple, Lord Claud Hamilton, Lord James Elphinstone and Lord Eglinton. The Queen of Scotland (Anne of Denmark) was also a Catholic convert. Letters from the Scottish Nobles to King Philip are given among the *Spanish State Papers,*

as well as a letter from Bernardino de Mendoza to them (pp. 427 and 615–6).

Two *Memoranda* dated 1601, by the *Earl of Bothwell, Admiral of Scotland*, append a list of the names "of the Catholic gentlemen of the north who will join our fleet coming from Flanders". They are as follows:

Earl of Caithness } my brothers
Viscount Murehill }
    „   Mackay
Earl of Sutherland
Viscount Mackintosh
Marquis of Huntly
Earl of Errol
    „   Athol
Viscount Inchaffray
Earl of Gowrie
Viscount Ogilvie
    „   Gray
Baron Burleigh
    „   Balcarres

Names of the lords of the west and border who will join our fleet—

Duke of Lennox	Viscount Paisley
Viscount Semple	„ Sanquhar
Baron Fleming	„ Maxwell
Marquis of Angus	„ Herries
Baron Buchanan	„ Hume
„ Rastellerse (?)	Baron Ferinhurst
Viscount Livingston	„ Roslyn
„ Seton	The Earl of Bothwell's
	Horsemen

(C.S.P.S., pp. 679–80.)

A formal and chilly *Report of the* [Spanish] *Council of State on the aforegoing letter of the Earl of Bothwell* states that there is no possibility of his proposed expedition taking place and concerns itself with a possible pension from Philip to the Earl.

6. From a position of comparative obscurity the small Kingdom

K

of Scotland had, since 1560, become one of the main pivots of the Counter Reformation. By a rare combination of circumstances she, like Ireland, had been thrust into the heart of the European religious, national and political vortex.

But it is in the personal history and character of James VI that we must look for the answer to the enigma of the resuscitation and then the languishing of the Catholic faith in Scotland, with its reactions on the shipwrecked Spaniards. Forcibly separated from his mother Mary, Queen of Scots, as a small child, he had been crowned on his mother's enforced abdication, in 1567. In 1587, the pawn of violently opposed religious and political parties, and a martyr to her faith Mary had been beheaded in the year preceding the coming of the Armada. Her death, in fact, was one of the precipitating causes for its arrival.

After his mother's execution it was hoped that James, who had been reared a Protestant, would commit himself to Catholicism since his Catholic cousin, Esmé Stuart, Sieur d'Aubigny and later Duke of Lennox, had swayed him emotionally in this direction at the age of fifteen. Lennox assured the Pope that James would be instructed at home or abroad, that he himself would be responsible for raising a foreign force to enable the lad to overthrow the tyranny of the Scottish Kirk and the Protestant Lords, who were attempting to throttle his uncertain power. Precariously balanced over against these were the ancient Catholic nobility who looked upon Protestantism as a dangerous but possibly fleeting heretical experiment.

At the age of sixteen James had been kidnapped, but a year later, in 1583, he had escaped from his Protestant captors to begin his difficult personal rule of a torn and distracted realm. The conflicting elements and trends in Scotland, both religious and political, were mirrored in his own vacillations and contrivings to balance opposing forces. By nature he became increasingly cautious, cunning, even shifty. Of acute intellect he had, perforce, a pliant conscience and became a past-master at deception to save his head. His overriding intention was to inherit the throne of England and to this end he subserviated all his energies. What combination could best guarantee him this throne? He had, on the one hand, to keep peace between the powerful Scottish lords of opposing faiths; to placate Rome; to falsely encourage the Jesuits to whom he was in part drawn and to whom he craftily entrusted diplomatic missions and secret messages for the Pope, France and Spain. At all costs Elizabeth must be reassured and the powerful Kirk, backed by her ministers, mollified. Thus he blew now hot, now cold. Where before he had favoured the Jesuits next he cut the ground from under their feet by making open proclamations against them, and by accepting a pension from Elizabeth after forming an avowed alliance with her, two years before the Armada set sail in 1586.

He was perfectly aware that his seduction to either side was a major theme and task of the Counter Reformation. Timid and fearful by nature he was flattered by the inflation which such a role involved. In 1592 he was oddly benevolent to the most distinguished of Scottish Catholic plotters and sent for the Jesuit Provincial to carry a message to the Pope offering toleration to the Catholics, and asking for the creation of a Scottish Cardinal. The latter move was a counter stroke against the intolerable power of the Presbyterians insisting on sanctions against the Catholic peers. By a neat and effective blow he ultimately secured the subjection of both the Catholic Earls and the Kirk of Scotland, in 1597, but these matters are beyond the period under consideration.

Many of the Catholic people, reduced to a state of confusion, lassitude, and disillusion, seeing that many priests had become preachers, abandoned their faith. But those in the extensive Highlands and the Isles, that is in the north and south-west, remained predominantly Catholic, subject in places to persistent persecution as late as the mid-nineteenth century.

Captain de Cuellar's dismissal of James as "a nobody in his own country" without effective power or authority is superficial. He underestimated James' natural talent for duplicity and endurance under constant pressure from opposing forces. He seems unaware that on occasions, when he thought it safe or when it suited him,

James had generously aided the shipwrecked Spaniards. After the loss of *La Trinidad Valencera* we have two corroborative proofs of this. The ship's Master reports that, of the survivors who made their way to Scotland, "the King had them clothed and some alms given to them" (C.S.P.S., p. 492), and the two Spanish servants state that, after having reached Scotland:

> they proceeded on their way, being guided by men sent from one gentleman to another, until they arrived in Edinburgh, where the King was. By his orders they were kept lodged in the town for 30 days, being fed and clothed the while. He then sent them to France, dividing them amongst four Scottish ships which, as the weather was against them, had to coast along the English shore, and twice had to cast anchor in English ports. On one occasion the Governor of the place, learning that there were Spaniards on board the ships, sought to take them out, but the shipmasters said that the soldiers had been delivered to their care by the King of Scotland to carry to France, and had ordered them, on pain of death, not to abandon them. They therefore refused to surrender them, but would defend them with their own lives. They sent a boat to acquaint the King of Scotland of the occurrence, and he informed the Queen of England that, as the Spaniards had appealed to him, he had provided ships to take them across, and he begged that they should not be molested in her ports. She therefore gave orders that they were not to be interfered with. Twenty days had passed in the meantime, the weather having still detained them in port, but at last they set sail and all arrived in France.

They add that some of the Spanish nobles provided them with "50 crowns for their journey" (C.S.P.S., p. 509).

This *Statement*, made on January 21st, 1588–9, but referring to events in the previous autumn and early winter, provides a contrast to de Cuellar's subsequent treatment in Scotland and his adventures in crossing to the continent. Evidently Burghley and Elizabeth's other ministers had hardened in their attitude towards the role that Spain was continuing to play against Protestant England. This toughening policy is reflected in the callous behaviour of both O'Cahan and James VI. As the measures of England increased in severity so did those of the Irish princes and Scottish King, half in league with and anxious to placate Her Majesty.

7. Alexander Farnese, Duke of Parma, was the nephew of King Philip and Governor General in the Netherlands, over which his mother and grandfather had ruled before him. Philip had done wisely to place him there for the Netherlands were his passion. He set to work to order and subdue the rebellious discontented peoples who had groaned under and revolted against the weight of Spanish taxation and the Duke of Alba's bloody rule.

A brilliant military strategist, "easily the first captain of his age" and the "best general in Europe" (Mattingly, p. 81), he had, like Medina Sidonia, prophesied the failure of his uncle's grandiose scheme of conquering England through a mating of unwieldy sea-and-land forces in the right, the necessary, nick of time. For Parma had his own nautical and military difficulties, including a strike of local workmen who "downed tools" and refused to get on with building the flat-bottomed barges essential for embarking the invading troops (C.S.P.S., pp. 236–8). Parma had even suggested dispensing with the fleet altogether and, like Buonaparte and Hitler, had envisaged invading England with flat-bottomed barges which, favourable winds and tides permitting, would safely carry their cargo of 30,000 men and 4,000 cavalry. These would put out from Nieuport and Dunkirk in a single moonless night. Philip with his tireless pen had scotched this plan in a single succinct phrase—"Hardly possible".

But at all costs it behoved him to be obedient to his uncle and to attempt to supplement his infinitely-plotted scheme with his own brilliant military gifts. He dutifully made his way to Dunkirk to command operations. But nature was not compliant. The high tides of spring which would have floated him off the Dunkirk sandbanks were not available on August 5th when the fleet approached Calais Roads. The full moon of August was on the 17th: that of July had passed on the 18th. The tide was neap and Parma's fleet had missed both. (See p. 33 of J. Holland

Rose's *Was the Failure of the Spanish Armada due to Storms*, Proc. of the Brit. Acad., Vol. XXII, London, 1937, where he gives the dates (O.S.) from information supplied by the Observatory, Cambridge.)

The Scottish nobles were in constant touch with him through trusted secret messengers. The Earl of Huntly, Robert Bruce and Colonel Semple wrote to Parma in August, September and November, 1588, but there is no record among the *State Papers Spanish* of any letter written on behalf of de Cuellar and the other shipwrecked Spaniards in Scotland, during their prolonged stay there throughout the spring and summer of 1589. The noble-mens' letters reveal the Scottish Catholics' longing to join forces with Philip against England, and they contain references to the "disturbed state of the country" (Scotland), "never in so favour-able a condition for being conquered as at present, owing to the disputes that exist" (C.S.P.S., p. 362).

In September 1588, they considered that "things have changed for the worse" and state that

> they would have seized the King [James] if they had [had] means to resist the power of England or had [had] any assurance that aid would be sent to them.

They also pressed

> certain points . . . that their country is not like other States, solid and stable, where no changes can be brought about except after great preparations. In Scotland any accident will bring about a change, as the realm is so divided and dis-membered, and anyone attacking it with force is assured of victory, as there are no strong towns, and but few fortresses. The country is in such a condition that it cannot but wait for the slow Spanish resolutions; and if the Lords are to be utilized action must be accelerated, as affairs in Scotland change. (C.S.P.S., pp. 427–8.)

By November Robert Bruce told the Duke of Parma that:

> his Catholic Majesty [Philip] and his successors have now the best opportunity that has ever presented itself of making

themselves rulers of this island, if it be not neglected. (C.S.P.S., p. 478.)

Knowing the Armada to have been blown north round Scotland, and driven onto the Irish coasts, the Duke of Parma determined to break up his camp in Dunkirk early in September, 1588.

They say [he] has retired from Dunkirk, having dismissed the Governor and replaced him. (Letter from a Genoese spy, September 7, 1588. C.S.P.S., p. 420.)

Dunkirk and Nieuport were the chief channel ports of Flanders, at this time part of the Spanish (southern) Netherlands, whereas Zeeland was one of the seven united provinces of the Dutch Republic, to the north. By now Elizabeth regarded it as "a first charge on her slender war-budget to see that French and Dutch independence were maintained against Philip". (G. M. Trevelyan, *History of England*, p. 355, London, 1943.)

After Parma's withdrawal Dunkirk was open to occupation by Protestant forces—from Holland and England, with possible reinforcements from Germany and France. There is evidence, however, that there were Spanish residents and travellers in it more than a year after the Armada had sailed.

8. The gold ducat was worth about nine shillings and fourpence and the silver ducat of Italy about three shillings and sixpence, but its value varied from country to country and decade to decade.

9. In August 1585, the Duke of Parma had conquered the ten southern Netherland provinces and cracked Antwerp, the commercial metropolis of northern Europe, forcing her to surrender. Having suffered from the massacres under the Duke of Alba her population by 1590 was depleted by one-fourth. It was to the merchants of Antwerp that the Duke of Parma looked for loans when part of his army, the most formidable in Europe, forged out of a heterogeneous collection of mercenaries, was garrisoned in the Netherlands: and it was to Antwerp that he went in 1588 when he received a letter from the Queen of England which, it

was rumoured, treated of peace, lodgings for her commissioners being prepared in the town (C.S.P.S., pp. 238 and 202).

What became of the *San Pedro*, the galleon of Castile on which de Cuellar set out as Captain? A Spanish ship of this name, losing her bearings after escaping the perils of the Irish coast, piled up at what the shipwrecked Spaniards called Hope in their statement, that is Bolt Tail in Devon (not Cornwall, as the Index to the *State Papers Spanish* give it). But this was the *San Pedro el Mayor*, from the squadron of hulks commanded by Juan Gomez de Medina. She was carrying the wounded and some of these men, about eighty-three in number, survived illness and shipwreck to be taken prisoner by Sir William Courtenay, a man so powerful in Devon that the local justices refused to treat with him when the half-starved prisoners, who had appealed to the Queen in writing, broke out of confinement and turned to the justices for redress. Sir William demanded extortionate prices for their ransom, and bickering over these men went on until 1592 between Sir William and the Queen, who allowed him to retain fifteen of the men, and Sir William and a Breton Duke.

But nowhere, in any of the published pages on the Armada, is there a reference to the fate of de Cuellar's galleon. She is not listed among the ships lost in battle, or off the Scottish or Irish coasts. This does not prove that she did *not* founder, or was *not* wrecked, since the lists are inaccurate and incomplete, and because some of the lost ships remain unnamed to this day. It is possible that she got home to Spain. But this would have been small consolation to de Cuellar, whose ship had been taken from him, and who had escaped death so narrowly and so frequently after separation from her.

5

Victims and Survivors of Note

Recalde, Aramburu, and the Prince d'Ascoli; Don Alonso de Leyva, Don Alonso de Luzon and Don Luis de Cordova.

THERE were, of course, other Armada survivors in Ireland as well as de Cuellar, other shipwrecked men whether great aristocrats like Don Alonso de Luçon, who spent long years in captivity before negotiations for his ransom were effected, or rough seamen and soldiers whose recorded examinations make moving reading among the *English State Papers* of the period. Many of these did not survive long. They were put to the sword soon after the information desired was extracted from them. Many more died without even being captured. Others, like the Duke of Medina Sidonia, the unwilling Captain General of the Ocean Sea, and the Almirante General, Recalde, got home with their wracked ships and starving diseased men, some to die on landing, others before ever they entered port. Some, like the men from the crippled *Zuñiga*, deserted at Le Havre where this galleass put in for repairs, and either made their way homeward slowly or, crafty and vagrant, remained expatriate for fear of imprisonment, punishment or death.

A fortnight before de Cuellar was wrecked off the Sligo coast, further south, off the Blaskets, another Spaniard—Marcos de Aramburu, Paymaster and Controller of the Galleons of Castile —was undergoing harassing experiences at sea. His ship was the *San Juan Bautista*, Vice-Flagship of this squadron, not to be confused with another ship of the same name in the same squadron, under Admiral Diego Flores de Valdés. Aramburu's ship had the good fortune to escape shipwreck by a hair's-breadth.

His account begins when the fleet was off Rockall and ends in Spain. It has not, as yet, been translated in full and the passages quoted herein are from a translated portion that concerns his adventures off the Kerry coast only.[1] The whole first appeared in print in Fernandez Duro's *La Armada Invencible*, in 1885. Aramburu's narrative is of great value in that it gives us details of his and the Almirante General's, Recalde's, experiences off the most westerly headland of Europe and that haunting cluster of islands, the Blaskets, whose Gaelic name so perfectly describes them as shells, scaled off from the mainland.

The adventures of the Spanish ships off the Blaskets (variously spelt by the Elizabethans Blasquets, Blaskenes and Blasgay) and in the Sound, called *Sunda* by the Spanish, are amongst the most fully documented of all those off the Irish coasts. This is not to be wondered at, for when at last the identification of one of the ships filtered through to the English, and it was learnt that she was none other than the Fleet Vice-flagship with Recalde on board, that is the *San Juan of Portugal* (a galleon of 1,050 tons carrying 50 guns and a complement of 500 soldiers and sailors when she set out) excitement at the possibility of capturing her, her treasure, and the Admiral worth a kingdom in ransom, mounted high.

The *San Juan* was, however, sadly broken and depleted by the time she reached the Blaskets. She had seen fierce and bitter service up Channel and in the Narrow Seas, had had her mainmast shot through and through and was losing five men a day through lack of water and clean food. The Admiral himself had taken to his bed long since and only arisen when, like an old war horse, he smelt out that part of the Irish coast with which he was familiar through previous service, to bring his ship safely in to one of the most dangerous of all the harbours of the west. For Recalde, in 1580, had helped to escort the Spanish and Irish Papal forces, bearing a second Bull to the oppressed and dis-

[1] *Armada Ships on the Kerry Coast*, Rev. W. Spotswood-Green, Proc. of the Royal Irish Academy, Vol. XXVII, Sec. C, pp. 263-9, Dublin and London, 1908-9, hereafter given as *Aramburu*.

tressed faithful in Ireland. These men were savagely butchered at the Fort of Gold, the *Dun an Oir* as the Irish has it, by the command of the then Lord Deputy, Lord Grey of Wilton—after a siege by land and water in which Captain Walter Raleigh was concerned since he was in charge of a company of men. So barbarous and treacherous was the annihilation of the foreign forces that for half-a-century or more afterwards the phrase *Graii fides* denoted the vilest perfidy, the name of Grey becoming synonymous for this, rather as Quisling has done in our own day.

The first written information conveyed to the English concerning the (unnamed) *San Juan of Portugal* and accompanying ships was in an undated letter sent to Vice President Norreys of Munster by Dominic Ryesse (Rice—and there was an Irish pilot, so named, with the Armada), the Suffrein, or Sovereign, of Dinglecush.

> Spaniards in the Sound of Blasgay. A Scotchman taken prisoner by them reports them sick, destitute of victual, and in great extremity for want of knowledge. A great galleass [sic] with 1,000 men.[1]

This was promptly forwarded by Norreys to Walsyngham on September 8th/18th. Not until ten days later did the Lord Deputy Fitzwylliam and the Council forward to the Privy Council in England a batch of *Briefs, Examinations* and *Reports* concerning the (by then) numerous wrecks and sightings of Spanish ships off the western coast. Among them Sir Richard Byngham's announcement of "Three ships cast away at Sligo", together with James Traunte or Trant's (the English government undertaker at Dingle's) astonishing announcement on September 11th/21st to Sir Edward Denny (who had already put to death the twenty-four men sent out from the Castilian ships courteously requesting friendship and information), which was as follows:

> Three great ships, one of 900 tons (sic), being the Admiral's, who is *John* Martines de Ricaldo (sic), ride at anchor betwixt the Fereter's main island [the Great Blasket] and the shore.[2]

[1] C.S.P.I., pp. 26–7.   [2] Ibid., p. 42.

Norreys, at Shandon near Cork, had assured Walsyngham that he had taken the news of the Spaniards lying in Blasket Sound seriously, and was "going towards the Spaniards with 200 foot and 50 men". It was these men, no doubt, with other local 'affected' Irish, who took Recalde's first scouts prisoner; but, as we shall see, the seasoned old Admiral, although he was deathly ill, eluded capture.

Aramburu's account of trouble off the Kerry coast begins on September 11th/21st, the same day as Trant's announcement. During this time his ship, the *San Juan Bautista*, had been beating about uncertain islands off the Norse-named Dorsey or Dursey Head, surmised to be either the Skelligs of the Saints, or the Ox (today called the Bull) and Cow. The weather was atrocious, with fickle winds of great force and mounting seas. Other Spanish ships appeared and disappeared through mists and in great darkness; sometimes they were recognized and sometimes not. The *Trinidad*, another Castilian ship of the same squadron, at first sailed close to them, then the *San Juan Bautista* bore down on another "big ship with a tender" for whom Aramburu's galleon charitably kept her lantern burning all night. At daybreak of the 15th two more vessels were sighted to windward and to leeward, the first going north and showing light, the second with no lantern burning.

> We suspected that they were the same as those of the previous evening, and that they were trying to get away from the land, of which we too were in dread.[1]

Suddenly they recognized the two ships to be none other than Recalde's great *San Juan* and an accompanying tender.

> We turned towards him, despairing, with the wind athwart . . . ignorant of the coast, or of any remedy [to escape being wrecked thereon].

To their astonishment they saw Recalde turn east, doubling one of the Blasket islands to the north, which they had now reached without being sure of which they were, the mainland lying

[1] This and unspecified ensuing quotations—*Aramburu*.

suspiciously near. Believing that the San Juan had information to give her the San Juan Bautista followed, standing to windward. But the San Juan

> kept approaching the land [fearful to them] and ran into the port of Vicey [Inishvickillaun] through an entrance between low rocks, about [as wide as] the length of a ship, and so anchored. We came in behind her, and after us the tender. This [the course] was shown [to Recalde] by a Scotsman whom he had on board his ship, whose vessel the Duke had taken. This day we saw another ship to leeward close to hand.

With these plain words Aramburu describes Recalde's brilliant feat of warping into and anchoring in this sound of fierce tides and submerged rocks. It appears that he passed close to Inishtooskert, the northern island, and to the north of the islet Carrigfadda where, with a westerly wind "he might have failed to luff up to the anchorage", which would have meant destruction on the dark leeward cliffs.

Who was the mysterious nameless Scotsman? This is the second time that he has appeared in official reports, first in the Sovereign of Dinglecush's report and now in Aramburu's narrative. No writer on the Armada seems to have been interested in him, or how he came to be on board Recalde's San Juan. We find him a third time in the fuller transcriptions of prisoners' examinations given by (Sir) John Laughton.

> He saith that there was an English pilot with the Duke [of Medina Sidonia] . . . and that the Scot was taken in the north part [the Norway Channel] after the English fleet had parted from them [the Spanish fleet, on the 12th of August past the height of Berwick] in a ship of 500 ton, in which was about twelve men, which the fleet hath carried with them, both the ship and the men. Six of the Scots were aboard the Admiral [the San Juan of Portugal], whereof one is he that is taken.[1]

[1] C.S.P.I., p. 39 and Laughton II, pp. 225–6. Admiral in Spanish is used for both the officer and his ship.

The man who is giving testimony is a Biscayan mariner, John de Licornio of Lekyte, Lekite, or Licket (Lequeitio), aboard Recalde's Fleet Flagship, and obviously one of the first scouts sent out by Juan Martinez in search of water, fresh food and information. Licornio's simple sentences imply the need of the Spaniards for local fishermen or traders, often as good as pilots, who knew the Scottish and Irish coasts, which the Armada had never expected, or been victualled, to round. That, like some great spider, the *San Martín* should put out her tentacles and seize a (presumably) Scottish ship with her dozen men shows how rapacious the Spaniards could be when in need of guidance and information. They had not hesitated to take up an English ship when off Plymouth but we are not told that, having got the information they required, they did not let both ship and men go.

We know that a single ship, the fleet flagship, the great *San Martín*, had as many as four pilots, one of them English. Duro's list of pilots with the Armada gives the names of two other men who appear to be Irish and Scottish—Guilermo (William) Brian (O'Brien) and Juan (John) Gordon.[1]

(Sir) Martin Hume singled out eighteen of the 238 salaried officers with the fleet as appearing "to have been either Irish or English".[2] Five Irishmen "lost with the Spanish army" and four at the Spanish court are named by one Christopher Arthur, a merchant of Limerick, recently come out of Spain in the spring of 1588–9, one being a merchant of Drogheda and another bearing the curious name of *John of all Johns*. Arthur closes by stating that there were at that time

> 15 gallies in St. Mary Port [in Andalusia], 12 in Lisbon and two in Seville. These are probably Spanish ships preparing for the Indies or for the next feared venture of Philip against Ireland or England.[3]

Because of the presence of Maurice Fitzgerald, titular Earl of Desmond, on board one of the Armada ships, together with

---

[1] Duro II, p. 201.
[2] C.S.P.S., p. 284.
[3] C.S.P.I., pp. 135–6.

some Irish officers, Froude presumed that the successful pilotage of some of the ships into safe anchorage—between the Great Blasket and the mainland, and in Scattery Roads—proves that these men were pilots. But does it? They were probably military officers, not pilots or navigators, and certainly not fishermen, traders or sailors.

Yet in spite of a formidable list of pilots when the Armada set out—most of them Spanish, Italian, or Portuguese—there seems to have been a shortage of experienced pilots. While the Spaniards made excellent Mediterranean sailors and had explored foreign seas, few of them had visited British waters: they could not be expected to intimately know the Scottish and Irish coasts unless they had at one time been fishermen or traders here.

On August 1st the Duke of Medina Sidonia frantically appealed to the Duke of Parma for trustworthy pilots when off the Flemish banks:[1] and at this very time when he had seized the Scottish ship, or just before, he promised a French pilot on Saturday, August 13th, that he would reward him with 2,000 ducats if he would bring him safely home to a Spanish port.[2]

Equally important is the admission of Don Pedro de Valdés, in command of the Andalusian squadron, his flagship being the captured *Nuestra Señora del Rosario*. Taken prisoner he was held for ransom for the space of five years and became something of a favourite, a "show piece" while in England. He was allowed to go hunting, dined in the City with the Lord Mayor and Aldermen, boasted of his good relationship with Drake, corresponded with Lord Burghley, and was summoned to court by Queen Elizabeth. He remained in England until the spring of 1593, when he went to Brussels where he wrote to King Philip that the English, at court, were desirous of the "old friendship" with Spain.

His ship had surrendered after she had been crippled in the serious skirmish between Eddystone and Start Point on August 1st. Later, on being towed from Dartmouth to Chatham, she was

[1] & [2] C.S.P.S., pp. 358 and 447.

found to be so badly damaged that she was not worth repairing and was broken up.

Spanish accounts say that she sank on her way to Chatham but this does not appear to be the case.[1]

On August 4th Don Pedro was examined, when he made this extraordinary admission:

... he saith that they [the Armada] have few pilots, whereof the most part are Spaniards and unexpert; and that there are few mariners [sailors].[2]

This was his frank answer to the twenty-second of twenty-three questions on which he was asked to give evidence.

Medina Sidonia makes no reference to the captured Scottish ship, reported by Aramburu and others, but the Spanish ambassador in Paris gives further confirmation of this piratical seizure in a letter to King Philip:

A man who left Edinburgh on the 4th [of September], and came overland, says that the Scottish fishing-boats had returned home, reporting that they had passed the Spanish Armada between the Orkneys and the Shetlands whilst they were fishing. They say there were 120 great ships, such as they had never seen before, and many small ones. The Spaniards had taken what dried fish the fishing-boats had, paying very well for it, *and also some shipmasters and pilots.* All the English, and fishing-boats which were at the fisheries with them, had been captured by the Spaniards, and their crews put in irons; so that when the Armada left there it had nearly 300 sail, and the weather was so fine that it would very soon arrive in Spain. (Letter among the Paris Archives dated Sept. 24, 1588.)[3]

Nor is any mention made by the Duke, or Aramburu, of transferring one or more of the captured Scotsmen to the *San Juan of Portugal.* Changing over from ship to ship from time to

[1] C.S.P.S., p. 494, footnote.
[2] Laughton II, p. 29.
[3] C.S.P.S., p. 434. (Italics mine.)

time seems to have been customary even among those high in command. There is at least one reference to Medina Sidonia temporarily changing his ship when disease and conditions made the *San Martín* unbearable, since he probably considered his health and safety vital to that of the whole remaining Armada.

Licornio, the Biscayan seaman, with seven other men whom Recalde had sent out as scouts, was taken prisoner by the English soldiers waiting like hoodie crows on the tops of the dark cliffs of carboniferous sandstone near Dunquin. He was handed over to James Trant, the English agent, who reported the prisoners' arrival to the hated Sir Edward Denny in Tralee, and examined in Dingle. After this they, too, were probably "put to the sword" since they were not important enough for ransom, and if preserved would be both a source of nuisance and danger to the English if they had to be guarded with scant forces, or escaped, as one Spanish prisoner held for ransom had earlier done from Denny—hence his especial hatred for all men of this race.

To return to Aramburu—he confirms the surmise that Licornio and his companions were sent out to scout for water and supplies of food. On September 16th, he says, his ship and Recalde's made friendly exchanges. Recalde sorely needed an anchor of 30 cwt. which the *San Juan Bautista* had and did not require, in return for which he sent across two cables and a smaller anchor.

> On the 17th, Juan Martinez [the Admiral] sent a large boat with 50 arquebusiers to look out for a landing place on the coast, to collect information, and to treat with the Irish for a supply of water which was badly wanted, and of meat. They found nothing but steep cliffs on which the sea broke; and on the land some 100 arquebusiers were waving a white flag with a red cross on it [the plain St. George's flag, the English flag of the day, flown by every English ship]. It is surmised that they were English, and that *eight men* whom Juan Martinez sent on the 15th in a long-boat to reconnoitre were taken prisoner by them, or had perished at sea.

Among the eight men taken prisoner four were examined—Licornio; two Portuguese sailors, Emmanuel Fremoso on the

Admiral's ship, and Emanuel Francisco also aboard her it would seem; and a Fleming, Peter O'Carr, who wrongly states that the *San Juan* was of 900 tons, 150 short. Fremoso's evidence is the longest. Beginning with the sailing of the fleet from the Groyne he continues with his recital of the *San Juan* and the Armada's adventures, stating that the Vice-flagship had been disabled in the battle in the Narrow Seas—her foremast had been shot through by two cannon balls, and that they, "the greatest ships of the whole navy", were in the worst plight for food as they had hoped to take on supplies sent out to them by the Duke of Parma, although she had been "one of the best furnished for victuals" at her sailing. He states that twenty-five of the sailors are Basques and forty Portingals (Portuguese), many of the men and the Captain sick, "all very weak, and do lie down and die daily".

> There is in this admiral [the ship] left but 25 pipes of wine, and very little bread; and no water, but what they brought out of Spain, which stinketh marvellously; and their flesh meat they cannot eat, their drouth is so great. He saith no part of the navy, to his knowledge, ever touched upon any land, until such time as they came to this coast at Dingle-i-couch; nor hath had any water, victual, or other relief, from any coast or place sithence the English fleet left them.[1]

Francisco, examined, confirms that the *San Juan*'s mast

> is so weak . . . as they dare not abide any storm, nor to bear such sail as otherwise [s]he might do.

Having agreed with Fremoso's recital he states even more roundly that

> those in the ship that he is in do say that they will go *into the ground* [be buried] sooner than they will come such a journey again. . . . For himself he would not pass into Portugal again if he might choose, for that he would not be constrained [urged or impressed] to such another journey.

Previously:

[1] C.S.P.I., pp. 219–24. (Italics mine.)

The best that be in the Admiral's ship are scarce able to stand; and if they tarry where they are any [length of] time they will all perish.[1]

The third examinate, the Fleming, gives additional information about the Duke of Medina Sidonia whom the English were hoping to take captive:

They lost the Duke upon the coast of Norway . . . [he] is by this time in Spain, unless he be taken upon the seas; and ever after his departure from the English fleet [he] intended to go back to Spain, being frightened and dismayed. [The Duke did not reach Santander until September 22nd.]

Re-examined on September 12th, O'Carr states that the Admiral,

after such time as the fight was at Calais, came not out of his bed till this day sennight, in the morning that they came upon this shore.

He saith that this Admiral is of Biscay, either of Bilbao or Laredo, and of 62 years of age, and a man of service.

He says nothing of how much Recalde was trusted and loved by his men, but this is not the sort of evidence one gives when facts only are demanded, and the sword waits at the end of one's testimony. O'Carr closes this second examination with a confirmation that the Prince d'Asculy "passed from them in a pinnace about Calais".[2]

That Recalde went on taking in water in spite of the watchfulness and threats of the English soldiery, and the helplessness of the Irish under their surveillance, has long been a tradition. The account of Aramburu confirms the belief:

The 18th, 19th and 20th we remained in the same port without being able to get out. Juan Martinez went on taking in water: and I having no long-boat or other boat, could do nothing; and he but little, and that with much labour.

[1] C.S.P.I., pp. 224-5.
[2] Ibid., pp. 226-9.

Now to take in water in broad daylight with the English soldiers watching would be impossible: the steep cliffs, too, would prevent his men. Dunquin is the only small hard-won harbour along this part of the Kerry coast from Smerwick to Ventry, and it is therefore out of the question for this exploit. The little strand of Coomeenoole, to the south of the headland of Dunmore, the most westerly in Europe, would seem the only possible spot. Here there is a freshwater stream, to which the cows of the neighbouring fields and the hamlet under Mount Eagle come down to drink, their footprints in the sand interspersed with those of barefoot boys who come to drive them up again. The only other possible strand is Ferriter's Cove to the north, and this would be further for the long-boats to row to under surveillance.

After this, Aramburu's account is taken up with the wreck of *Nuestra Señora* or *Santa Maria de la Rosa*, almost invariably mis-named in the *Examinations* of prisoners and confused by later writers with *Nuestra Señora del Rosario*, mentioned above. *La Santa Maria de la Rosa* was the vice-flagship of Oquendo's Guipuzcoan Squadron, a ship of 945 tons compared to the 1,150 of *Nuestra Señora del Rosario*. While Recalde's *San Juan*, in the violent westerly gale of September 21st off the Blaskets, drifted down on to the *San Juan Bautista*, smashing her lantern and the tackle on her mizzen-mast, to their bewilderment another Spanish ship came into the Sound at mid-day by a north-westerly entrance—none other than the *Santa Maria de la Rosa*, firing her guns "as if asking [for] help".

She had all her sails torn to ribbons, except the foresail. She anchored with a single anchor, as she had no more. And as the tide, which was coming in from the south-east, beat against her stern, she held on till two o'clock, when it began to ebb, and at the turn she commenced drifting, about two splices of cable from us, and we with her; and in an instant we saw she was going to the bottom while trying to hoist the foresail, and immediately she went down with the whole crew, not a soul escaping—a most extraordinary and terrible occurrence. We were drifting down on her to our perdition.

Aramburu, witness of this nightmare experience, was wrong in stating that no man survived. A sole survivor got ashore on a baulk of timber—a Genoese seaman, often called the son of the pilot because of a confused phrase in his statement—variously named Antonio de Monana, Don Antonio Meneses, or simply John Anthony of Genoa. In his examination it is he who gives the seemingly veracious details of the drowning of the Prince d'Asculo in this ship, even describing his elaborate clothing. He gives, too, the names of various high-born princes and aristocrats; the quantities of gold, silver, gold-and-silver-plate, the number of cannons of the field, the pieces of brass and cast iron belonging to the ship, and the number of "tuns of sack—50".[1]

The Reverend Spotswood-Green, who made a study of the cause and site of the sinking of the *Santa Maria*, suggests that they were one and the same—the rock now called Stromboli, which "may then have been awash". This rock, when he was writing in 1909, then had

> two and a half fathoms on it at low water. . . . It seems to have been smashed when *H.M.S. Stromboli* struck it some fifty years ago. The small brass cannon fished up "about 70 years ago" by the Blasket islanders came either from the *Santa Maria* or the *San Juan* 'of Ragusa'.

Yet another distressed ship came in to anchor—the *San Juan* 'of Ragusa' with her mainmast gone: "it was impossible to help her". Rising seas angered by the fierce tides ebbing against the wind; submerged rocks; dragging anchors which, when they drew them up, had shanks broken off from the stock, "and the cable chafed by the rocks over which we were lying"; and the general state of disrepair in which the ships were after battles with the English; the cold winds and rain, drought and disease all caused the loss of these tormented ships, and great suffering to the ill and dying men on the ships that got away.

Both Recalde and Aramburu got home to Spain. The latter, with the Admiral's permission, sailed out first, but not without

[1] C.S.P.I., p. 40.

L*

fearful adventures. Taking on the whole company of another distressed ship the *San Juan Bautista* left "Vicey" with a light easterly
wind which soon died down. They were at once in danger of
being cast away again since the strong current was carrying them
back on to the islands. When the wind got up again Aramburu
tells how they made a second attempt

> . . . we went out with top-gallant sails set, as far as the reefs
> which lie to the north; and there the wind fell calm again,
> while the tide was drifting us on to the land to the north
> between four islands and the reefs.

Once more they were forced to anchor.

> An hour after nightfall the wind began to blow from the
> south-east, and the ship to drift onto the islands, which are
> so rocky that no one coming on to them could be saved. . . .
> Weighing anchor we set sail, commending ourselves to Our
> Lord, not knowing whether there was any way out. A des-
> perate venture; with a dark and cloudy night we tried to
> get out to windward of the reefs but the current would not
> allow us, rather it was carrying us to our destruction. We
> turned and tried by an opening between the islands. The
> wind was freshening still more; there was a sea on, with
> heavy cloud and violent showers. . . .

Aramburu and his companions, like de Cuellar, commended
themselves to Our Lady.

After this, for two more days the *San Juan Bautista* struggled
to make headway, only eight leagues and sometimes less from
land. The wind could not make up its mind to stay in one
quarter, chopping from west to south-east-by-south to west-
south-west, and then with a sudden shift to south and south-
south-west again. By the 28th yet another gale had got up, this
time from the north-west, which tore the *Bautista*'s foresail into
ribbons, "not a thread of it remaining". In the tremendous rolling
of the ship, the rolling of the guns and the shifting of the ballast,
barrels and cables, the unrelenting seas struck them "in the waist,
so that we thought all was up with us". All the next day and the

day after that (the 30th) was spent in righting the ship, only to meet yet another gale. None the less the *San Juan Bautista*, and after her Recalde in his battered *San Juan of Portugal*, with their starving crews, miraculously succeeded in getting home.

On September 5th/15th, three days before the Sligo ships were sighted as "coasting along the coast", Spanish ships numbering either seven or eleven were reported as being "in the river of Limerick", that is the Shannon. This king of rivers, 170 miles long, is the largest in Ireland or Britain; its estuary, a drowned river valley, stretches sixty miles west of Limerick city and is tidal two miles above it. The reports of the arrival of the Shannon ships multiplied and caused as much fear and excitement as those off the Blaskets. Their arrival was announced eight different times by English and Irishmen in government employ—the Governor of Connacht, two sheriffs, two or more mayors, an Attorney General, and the Lord Chief Justice.

The ships were first said to be anchored at *Caryge-e-Colle*, or *Carrick-ne-Cowley*, or Carrigaholt, "20 miles from Limerick". Next, four are described as being at Lupus (Loop) Head. This pointed promontory north of the Shannon estuary, ravaged by the winds, is the most westerly extremity of Clare. Finally, on September 21st/October 1st, confusingly they are said to be at "*Raviskeith* on Thomond Side", that is the old kingdom of Thomond, north of the Shannon, ruled over by the O'Briens. (There is a description of Thomond in Burghley's hand among the State Papers.) This proves to be "the best roadstead in the lower Shannon, Scattery Roads", its old name having been *Inniskeith*, or *Cathy*.[1] Byngham here reports that two of the ships were lost, and one burnt—the Spaniards' custom when a ship was past repairing and they did not wish her to fall into English hands. This was the *San Marcos*, one of the galleons of Portugal under the command of Recalde that had earlier been badly mauled in battle. The Shannon ships rode at anchor for a week. By the 12th/22nd there was great rejoicing: "Happy news of the de-

[1] Spotswood-Green, p. 438.

parture of the Spaniards", and "God be praised, those seven ships are gone",[1] and again, the "happy news of the departure of the Spaniards" is joyfully forwarded at midnight from the Mayor of Limerick in the west to the Mayor of Waterford in the east. The three remaining great ships and the three despatch boats that had cleverly anchored in Scattery roads had set sail for Spain.

Two days before this, a little to the north, on the coast of Clare, two more ships were wrecked in broad daylight at two o'clock in the afternoon in Mal Bay. One has always been known simply as the "ship of St. Sebastian's". At first it would appear to have been the *Santa Ana* of Sebastian according to the testimony of an Irishman pressed aboard her, but when we look carefully we see that William Brown mentions his return

> with but two sail to Passage in Biscay after the great over-throw [defeat],[2]

so that it must be another ship from the same port which was wrecked off Milltown Malbay. She came ashore at "Donnbeg" (*the small fort*) with a loss of 300 men drowned.[3]

The second ship, said to be "of Flanders", attempted to get shelter behind Mutton Island and was wrecked beneath another 'castle' called *Tromra*. These ships were wrecked south of the Cliffs of Moher, composed of black millstone grit and dropping 600 feet sheer to the sea, a terrifying spectacle to those in danger at sea. Spanish Point, two miles west of Milltown Malbay, does not necessarily indicate the exact spot of the wrecks here, but possibly the place of the Spaniards' burial. It is said that more than 1,000 men perished, some by drowning on the reefs to the landward of Mutton Island, some by the sword of Boethius Clancy, and Sir Turlough O'Brien of Thomond, and others acting under orders of the English Governor. Mounds and boulders in fields bordering the shore are still marked out as graves of the unfortunate victims. Relics of the Spanish ships, said to have been numerous and to

[1] C.S.P.I., p. 38.
[2] Ibid., p. 64.
[3] Ibid., p. 38.

have existed "up to the early part of last century", have disappeared.

Another Spanish ship in danger off the Clare coast was the galleass *Zuñiga* whose adventures have already been related when, riding at anchor beneath Liscannor castle, she sent out a boat seeking provisions and information. Among the scouts sent out was, strangely enough, her purser, Petrus Baptista, who was taken prisoner and examined before the Bishop of Kildare. In 1591 a man with this name is reported as being a "servant of the Lord Deputy", and in the following spring he is mentioned by Lord Burghley.[1] If it is the same Baptista this is a singular case of a Spanish prisoner acting as a trusted agent for one of the English Governors.

Among the depositions and rumours spread by the wrecked Spanish sailors a very curious and interesting example of these is the report, frequently corroborated with seeming veracity, of the death of the so-called "base-born son" of Philip II—the Prince d'Ascule, Asculy, Asculi or Ascolo, whose title was taken from Asculum, the ancient town north-east of Rome. The *State Papers Ireland* give the important examinations of certain sailors with the Armada, all but one of whom, no matter what his nationality, agree in their conviction that the Prince was drowned off the Great Blasket Island.

The first we hear of him is on September 10th/20th from Pierre O'Carr, a Fleming:

> A bastard son of King Philip's is in this fleet [the Armada]. He is 24 years of age, and is called the Prince of Asculagh [sic], in Italy: he went in a ship with the Duke of Medina Sidonia. This Prince passed from them in a pinnace about Calais.[2]

Next, on September 11th/21st, the English agent at Dingle reports to Sir Edward Denny, the hated undertaker concerned with the massacre at *Dun an Oir*, and the murder of the twenty-

[1] Ibid., pp. 396 and 461.
[2] Ibid., p. 40.

four Armada Spaniards from Castile and Biscay who had surrendered to Lady Denny:

> Received his letter at Downequeyn [Dunquin]. . . . The Principe d'Ascula [sic], base son to the King of Spain, drowned with 500 tall [picked] men in the *Santa Maria de la Rosaria* (sic). The Duke himself is in the galleon *San Martín*.[1]

Next, from the examination of John Anthony of Genoa, mariner, elsewhere called de Monona, on September 15th/25th:

> The Spanish King's base son came in the company of the Duke of Medina Sidonia's ship, called the galleon of *San Martín*, of 1,000 tons, but at Calais where Sir Francis Drake came near them, this Prince went in a pinnace to the shore, and before his return the Duke was driven to cut his cables and let go his anchors and to depart, whereby the Prince could not recover that ship, but came into the ship called *Our Lady of the Rosary*. . . . [This is an error for *Our Lady of the Rose*.] His ship . . . struck on the rocks in the Sound of Blasquets. . . . All the company, 500, including the King of Spain's base son, the Prince of Asculo, drowned on Tuesday last, excepting only this examinate.[2]

Monona, like other shipwrecked men confused the two ships *Our Lady of the Rosary* and *Our Lady of the Rose*, or again it may have been the Welshman, David Gwynn, who interpreted the examinations of the prisoners, who made the error. For it was *Our Lady of the Rose* that went down dramatically in Blasket Sound, as the Paymaster of the Galleons of Castile, Aramburu, proves in his account, and not *Our Lady of the Rosary*. This latter ship was Pedro de Valdés' flagship of the Andalusian squadron, captured by the English in battle and ignominiously towed into dock, whereas *Our Lady of the Rose* was the vice-flagship of the Guipuzcoan squadron under Miguel de Oquendo.

All of these accounts were forwarded straightway to England, first by Sir Henry Wallop to Burghley, on September 16th/26th from Cork, and the last by the Lord Deputy and Council to the

---

[1] & [2] Ibid., pp. 42 and 40.

Privy Council on September 18th/28th, from Dublin. One writer states that Monona was examined before Sir William Herbert, President of Munster. Under him he even described what the Prince was wearing when he was drowned—"white satin, with russet silk stockings, his doublet and breeches cut after the Spanish mode".[1] He also graphically describes the appearance of the Prince—"of reasonable stature", having brown hair stroked upwards, a small beard, and a pale face "with some little red on his cheeks", and he gives his age as twenty-eight as against another examinate's statement that he was twenty-four. Such details sound remarkably accurate and trustworthy. One would not think it possible that a man as marked as King Philip's son, and a Commander in the fleet, on board the same ship as Monona, could be mistaken for another aristocrat of lesser rank.

Among the *State Papers Spanish* there are also reports of the drowning of the Prince d'Asculy, together with Admiral Juan Martinez de Recalde.[2] But we know that Recalde got home, and if one piece of information in this welter of confused reports can be wrong so may another. It seems that the first examinate points the way to the truth when he says that the Prince "passed from them [the Armada] in a pinnace about Calais": and Purser Pedro Coco Calderon, always an accurate and intelligent reporter, says in his lengthy *Statement* to King Philip:

> The same day [Sunday, 7th August] the Prince of Ascoli, with three servants and a chaplain, took a patache and... went to Flanders.[3]

We can corroborate this by the Prince's own *Letter to the King* [Philip] dated August 12th. The manuscript, much mutilated and with the writing almost undecipherable, is docketed *Estado 594* and appears to be genuine.

> On the 7th instant your Majesty's Armada was at anchor in Calais Bay, the enemy's fleet being a league distant from it.

[1] *Romantic Hidden Kerry*, Thomas O'Sullivan, Tralee, 1931, p. 64.
[2] C.S.P.S., p. 451 and other references.
[3] Ibid., p. 444.

At midnight, when the tide was running from the enemy's fleet towards us, they let loose seven fire ships, which came towards the Armada. The Duke of Medina Sidonia considered it necessary that the Armada should avoid these ships, and he accordingly directed some of us who were most in his confidence to go in zabras [Biscay smacks] and carry instructions to the other squadrons. By the Duke's orders I took with me Captain Marco, as I had done on other occasions, and sailed towards the rear squadron. In the interim the flagship [the *San Martín*] sailed away, and at daybreak I found myself in the midst of the enemy's ships, and our Armada too far away for us to reach it. Whilst I was in this position I saw a small pinnace in which were two majors who had been sent to carry orders through the Armada for the ships to put themselves into fighting trim. I therefore went on board the pinnace with the intention of making for the galleon, and we clapped on all sail with that object. Both wind and tide were against us, and the enemy were engaged with our fleet, so that I was cut off and in the rear of both fleets. I decided to follow in the wake of the fleets, but I was so hotly pressed by the boats which had attacked and defeated the galleass *Capitana* (*San Lorenzo*) that not a sailor could be induced to stir. Thus I remained all day until two o'clock next morning, when so violent a gale broke that I was obliged to run before it, I knew not whither, all that night without a pilot. In the morning I sighted Calais, but was too far to leeward to make it. I therefore had to enter this port [Dunkirk], where I found the Duke of Parma, and gave him an account of my proceedings, begging leave to return to the Armada. This he refused to allow. I am very unhappy to be out of whatever events may happen to the Armada, but as God has ordained otherwise, it cannot be helped, and my only wish is to be in some place where I may serve your Majesty and do my duty in a manner worthy of my birth. This I will always keep before me and on all occasions when my person may be of any service it shall be exposed to the death on your Majesty's behalf.

Dunkirk, 12th August, 1588.[1]

¹ C.S.P.S., pp. 378-9 and 450, footnote 2.

According to (Sir) Martin Hume the Prince lived many years after his ill-fated escapade.[1] He suggests that the confusion concerning his death may have arisen because his name was Antonio Luis de Leyva, implying that he was related to King Philip's favourite, Don Alonso de Leyva, who was to take complete command of the Armada if Medina Sidonia was disabled, and who was drowned on the rock of Bunboys. Can the Prince possibly have caught up with the fleet, as the Genoese mariner states, and come aboard Our Lady of the Rose, eventually wrecked off the Great Blasket? This seems unlikely as by Friday, August 12th, when he was writing to his alleged father from Dunkirk, the Armada had been blown as far north as 56°, "past the height of Hull, past the height of Berwick". And here the English pursuing ships "turned away and headed for the Firth of Forth",[2] which they feared the Spaniards might have entered in order to ally themselves with the Scots.

Yet the testimonies of the surviving Spanish sailors exist to bear witness to their belief that he was on board the ship wrecked with all-hands-but-one in Blasket Sound. Furthermore, if you ask a Dunquin man today 'who lies in the Spaniard's grave far from the rock-bound shore in a little coign of the hills' he will reply at once without hesitation, "'Tis the Prince d'Ascoli!" And when you protest that there are historians who deny the possibility he will retort with pride and exasperation:

"Don't be listening to those experts. We have the tradition."

If the Irish people, who reverence the resting-places of the dead, even the prehistoric, would permit archaeologists to excavate this disputed grave much might be revealed. It lies at the base of a track leading over Mount Eagle to Ventry, on an "island" made by two minute streams. It is a grave large enough to hold the bodies of several men, and the raised mound over it is still, after nearly four centuries, conspicuous. Some small stones are propped against its sides but it is in no way fenced or marked off, so that any person, not knowing what it is, may walk over

[1] C.S.P.S., pp. 378–9 and 450, footnote 2.
[2] Mattingly, pp. 288–9.

the grave. But all of the local people, even the children, know and respect it.

After close on 400 years Don Alonso de Leyva stands out as one of the most heroic and enticing figures with the Armada. He was Commander-in-Chief of the Light Cavalry of Milan under whose command the meticulous King Philip, confident of the success of the Armada forces in overcoming all obstacles and in landing at "Cape Margate", instructed the Duke of Medina Sidonia to place them in his *Supplementary Secret Instructions* from "I, the King" at Madrid, dated April 1st, 1588.[1] In case of the death or disablement of the Duke, Don Alonso was to take supreme command. Some idea of the prestige with which these great figures were surrounded is given us by the number of servants by which they were attended: the base-born son of Philip had thirty-nine, de Leyva thirty-six.[2]

By August 2nd when Medina Sidonia began to be enraged at the misfortunes of the fleet and its seeming lack of disciplined order and response, as they lay off Portland Bill he wrote to Don Hugo de Moncada, Commander of the Hulks, ordering the Armada to re-form in two squadrons, of which the rearguard was to be "reinforced by the best ships in the fleet, one half under the command of Martinez de Recalde, the most seasoned and renowned of all the officers afloat, and the other under de Leyva. On the 4th two of the tub-like hulks, who were in trouble and had fallen astern, were in danger of being captured by the English. Don Alonso came to their rescue with his flagship and two galleasses from the rearguard. One of the ships in distress was called *La Doncella*, the other was that very *Santa Ana*, the *Duquesa*,[3] which was later to "fall on the coast of Ireland" and to founder there after de Leyva had gone aboard her, when the *Rata* too had been wrecked and burnt. By the time that de Leyva had endured his first two castings ashore, and rumours had reached Philip of the loss of so many great ships off the west coast, the King was following their loss carefully and painfully.

1 & 2 C.S.P.S., pp. 249–50 and 284.
3 Ibid., pp. 442.

He notes in his own hand in the margin of a September *Statement from Ireland* (written in French but in an English hand) "This may be Don Alonso de Leyva".[1]

Long after this, in December of the same year, when confused reports of the wreck in October of de Leyva's third ship, *La Gerona*, began to come in from the Pilot General of the Armada, from the Spanish Ambassador in Paris, and from Spanish servants, the King was informed of how the *Duquesa* had been wrecked and how Don Alonso had fortified himself in the northwest of Ireland "in the province of Mac Win," that is at Loughros Mor in Donegal in the country of Mac Sweeny ne Doe. The agitated King once more writes in the margin—"Find out what province this is and let me know".[2] The last *Statement* in which de Leyva is mentioned is made by two servants with the Armada, Juan de Nova, a Galician, and Francisco de Borja from Antequera. The Spaniards give details of the wreck of the *Gerona*, stating that they learnt of her being "higher up the coast from an Irishman who spoke Latin," of how Don Alonso was got aboard on his chair, and how he "directed that they should return round Cape Clear [Erris Head] as they had no rudder and could not navigate".

They could, he thought, manage to get to Scotland, where they would obtain succour. They therefore went round Cape Clear and when they had arrived between the 'Spanish Sea' and the island of Scotland [the North Channel] they had a fair wind to carry them to Spain. The pilot therefore represented to Don Alonso that if he would allow him to set sail he would arrive in Spain in five days. Don Alonso replied that if he was sure the weather was favourable he could do so. But he was deceived in thinking that the weather was settled, for it changed and cast them upon the island of Ibernia [by which he means Ireland]. They ran upon a submerged rock and the galleass went to pieces, more than 1,300 men being drowned. Only nine sailors were saved, one of whom gave this statement.[3]

[1] C.S.P.S., p. 464.
[2] Ibid., p. 501.
[3] Ibid., pp. 509–10.

In a map of 1567 the 'Spanish Sea' is shown as the entrance to
the English Channel. Here de Nova means the Atlantic Ocean.
The Spaniards, except for the naval officers, had completely lost
their bearings.

I give this excerpt in full since it appears to explain—although
survivors' reports cannot always be trusted—the difficulty some
historians have had in deciding whether de Leyva intended, on
his final setting out to sea, to make for Spain or Scotland.

In searching for contemporary information about him and his
ships in the *State Papers Ireland* we come on that rare thing—an
Armada survivor's description of his bearing, appearance and
character, more graphic than any personal portrait drawn by
de Cuellar. This is provided by two sailors, the one Irish and the
other Cretan, who were examined, perhaps under torture, before
the Lord Deputy on December 29th, 1588, while on his protective and punitive journey through Connacht and the north. It is
accounts such as these that make dry State Papers leap to life,
since they embody corroborative evidence in a shorter form than
de Cuellar's own, and give an unconscious portrait of a man long
dead as valuable as one done in oils.

We have seen that there were several Irish sailors with the
Armada. This one, who was pressed into service against his will
at Lisbon on the "Flemish hulk St. Ann", that is *La Duquesa Santa
Ana*, had the high-sounding name of "James Machary of the
Cross, within the county of Tipperary". Perhaps he was really a
MacCarthy, or that *Macharg* whom Fernández Duro mentions
as an Irishman with the fleet. He was probably set down as "of
the Cross" (like the Spanish mystic) because he came from a
hamlet close by the great Cistercian Abbey, founded by Donal
O'Brien, King of Munster in 1168, on the banks of the beautiful
river Suir. The Abbey took its name from a fragment of the
True Cross given by the Pope to Murtagh O'Brien, an earlier
King of Munster, half a century earlier. Holy Cross, magnifi-
cently enshrining the relic, became one of the most renowned
places of pilgrimage in the British Isles.

Having stated how the *Santa Ana* fought in the Narrow Seas

(the English Channel) and later "fell upon the coast of Ireland in a haven called Erris St. Donnell [Erris Head]", Machary recounts the wreck of the *Rata Encoronada*, giving her complement of officers and men as he thought them to be, and how Don Alonso transferred on to the *Santa Ana*

> with all the goods they had in the ship of any value as plate, apparel, money, jewels, weapons and armour, leaving behind them victual, ordnance and much other stuff... which done, they set the ship on fire, and made sail for Spain, in which course, by a contrary wind they were driven back... to a place called Lougherris [Loughros Mor Bay].[1]

He continues with an account of the next disastrous storm which drove Don Alonso on to land once again, stating that he had been struck by a ship's capstan before being cast ashore so that "he was neither able to go [walk] nor ride", but was carried the nineteen miles overland, through the mountains to Killybegs where the *Gerona* lay, "between four men". Having previously been forced to encamp in two different castles or forts in Blacksod Bay, called Doona and Tirawn, then eight or nine days near Loughros Mor, Don Alonso encamped a further twelve or fourteen days at Killybegs until the *Gerona* might be repaired. Hearing of the approach of the Lord Deputy he put to sea for the third and final time, "having for his pilots three Irishmen and a Scot".

Machary of the Cross was not taken aboard and so was saved. The *Gerona* carried far too many men, the survivors of three wrecked ships determined to escape and get home at all costs, and places were required for the splendid aristocratic officers rather than humble seamen like Machary, who after all was now in his own country even though he had been "imprest" at the start. Thus he was now "thrust out of" the *Gerona*, one hopes to make his way home to the green plains of his native Tipperary after the fearful experience of being taken up and examined before Fitzwylliam.

---

[1] C.S.P.I., pp. 98–9. (See also Spotswood-Green, pp. 440–1.)

At the close of his examination there comes that flash of vivid description which re-creates Don Alonso de Leyva for us:

> He ... for his stature was tall and slender, of a whitely complexion, of a flaxen and smooth hair, of behaviour mild and temperate, of speech good and deliberate, greatly reverenced not only of his men, but generally of all the whole company.[1]

The use of the word *whitely* may be that of the man who set down the examination, but it is interesting to find it corroborated in that of the second Cretan seaman, George de Venerey of Candie (Candia, now Herakleion).

> Don Alonso was a whitely man with an Abram beard, but whether he was lame or not he knoweth not.[2]

Shakespeare uses the word, which means fair-skinned, in a marvellous thumb-nail sketch of an imagined wanton with a "whitely" face and "a velvet forehead, with two pitchballs for eyes stuck in her face". Don Alonso, so unlike the Englishman's usual conception of a black-haired, black-eyed Spaniard, may have come from the north of Spain where fair-haired types are more frequently found. The repeated enquiries by the authorities in England as to whether Don Alonso had survived and been taken prisoner, or perished, and the appearance of his name in the statements of Limerick and Waterford merchants who traded with and had been in Spain, indicate how important the English considered this distinguished and courageous soldier to have been. He received some kindness and sustenance in Ireland for an Irish priest, Terence O'Keynai, or O'Kenny, states that a Galway merchant, one James Blake, supplied him with victuals, in return for which Don Alonso gave him letters of recommendation to the King of Spain "who received him into great favour".[3]

Among other survivors of note—and the English were only interested in these for purposes of ransom, the common man not

[1] & [2] C.S.P.I., pp. 98–9.
[3] Ibid., p. 453.

counting a groat—were Don Alonso de Luçon whom we have already encountered aboard *La Trinidad Valencera* or when a prisoner at Drogheda, and Don Luis de Cordova, brother of the Marquis of Ayamonte, and the officers captured with them. "Reserved alive", like any stalled ox, Don Luis was taken prisoner from the *White Falcon* by Sir Murrough ne Doe O'Flaherty, in his country north of Galway Bay, who was forced to deliver him up to Byngham's brother, George. Thereafter he was an object of rival bargaining and dissension, the arguments and counter-arguments over him being directed finally by Byngham direct to the Queen, so angry was he at the Lord Deputy's arbitrary overruling of his own disposal of the captives. Among those saved, he wrote to her were:

divers gentlemen of quality and service, as captains, masters of ships, lieutenants, ensign-bearers, other inferior officers and young gentlemen, to the number of some fifty, whose names I have for the most part set down in a list, and have sent the same unto your Majesty; which being spared from the sword till order might be had from the Lord Deputy how to proceed against them, I had special direction sent me [by the latter] to see them executed, as the rest were only reserving alive one, Don Luis de Cordova, and a young gentleman, his nephew, till your Highness's pleasure be known. My brother George had one Don Graveillo de Swasso (sic) and another gentleman, by licence, and some five or six Dutch boys and young men who, coming after the fury and heat of justice was past, by entreaty I spared them, in respect they were pressed into the fleet against their wills. . . . But the Lord Deputy . . . made his way through this province, and in his passing along caused both these two Spaniards, which my brother had, to be executed, and the Dutchman and boys which were spared before, reserving none but Don Luis and his nephew, whom I have here [in the Castle of Athlone].[1]
Dec. 3rd/13th, 1588.

[1] Laughton II, pp. 299–301. (Also C.S.P.I., p. 77.)

Earlier, at the close of September under examination, Don Luis had given details of the Armada's progress from Plymouth up-channel, stating that he was "of Andalozia" [sic] and Captain of a Company.

He saith, touching himself, that his elder brother is a gentle-man of 1,000 ducats per annum, and that himself is not of any livelihood. He was employed by the King as a gentleman at 30 crowns per mensem in Cicilia [sic], and sent for from thence by the King to serve in this expedition, wherein he had charge of a hundred men in this ship that is cast away.[1]

In October he makes the curious allegation against the Irish of

letting the Spaniards range up and down the country after they had stripped them of their apparel and robbed them of their money and jewels.[2]

What would he have had them do? They were incapable of housing and feeding and restraining large numbers of men, since they themselves had been robbed of their lands and impoverished by the English since the previous generation. The only other alternative was to have had the Spaniards killed. Perhaps, being a soldier, he considered this the inevitable and better end.

On January 5th/15th Don Luis was despatched as a prisoner by the Lord Deputy from Dublin Castle to London together with Don Roderigo de Lasso de la Vega, "cavellero de la horden de Saint Iago" [sic], earlier listed as "sick" in the list of prisoners at Drogheda, on October 13th/23rd. With other distinguished Spaniards they were to be exchanged for "Monsieur de Nowe, and Tyllyny, his son". Of these curiously-named gentlemen or their significance we learn nothing. But in April 1591, Don Luis was still languishing in London, under the custody of Sir Horatio Palavicino, the Genoese banker knighted in 1587, who was heartily tired of dealing with them, their ransom and "diet". He is

much annoyed at not being able to receive the money due to him for this service, which amounts to 1,800 *scudi di sole*

1 & 2 C.S.P.I., pp. 50–1 and 62.

... and has written ... that he would take 1,000 *scudi di sole* for the same if he might be rid of the business.[1]

Written to Burghley by Giovanni Battista Giustiniano the letter was in Italian.

In the same year, on October 31st, Palavicino again sends in his overdue account, assessing the amount owing for "61 Spaniards taken in Ireland and sent into England" at £786.10.6,[2] equivalent to ten times as much today. Meanwhile the Lord Deputy also requested payment for the prisoners' ransom.

1 & 2 Ibid., pp. 390–433.

6

Aftermath

By the middle of October 1588, while de Cuellar was still in Ireland, Medina Sidonia with two-thirds of his fighting strength had led the broken fleet home to Spanish waters. Of the four pilots aboard the *San Martín* three had died at sea. We know that one of them was an Englishman. Was it he who

> brought the flagship staggering past Coruña before a westerly gale, and conned her to her landfall off Santander?[1]

The Duke, wracked with dysentery and starvation "stayed aboard six days after their arrival".[2] Too weak to sit upright in the pilot boat, when at last he got ashore he appeared to the astonished spectators, together with the fifty "gentlemen" who followed him, "all apparelled in black like mourners. The like lamentation was never in any country as in Biscay and Asturia". The dead men and those dying from scurvy or typhus, aggravated by hunger and thirst, were carried ashore and taken to their lodgings in waggons, or given sea-burial, while the countryside was once again scoured for fresh food, water and wine. Like that nightmare-scene re-created by Coleridge in *The Ancient Mariner* ships floated into harbour with men so weakened that they were unable to lower the sails or drop anchor, one of the ships sinking shortly after she made port.

That great seaman, Vice Admiral of the Fleet, Juan Martinez de Recalde, and Miguel de Oquendo, Commander of the Guipuzcoan Squadron, were both dead. Recalde, who had been ill for the greater part of the disastrous voyage, gallant, skilful Recalde beloved by his Biscayans, got home only to die four

[1] Mattingly, p. 312.
[2] C.S.P.I., pp. 126-7.

days after the *San Juan* had limped into Coruña on October 7th. According to the Master of the Rolls, Sir Nicholas White of Waterford, "there was great mourning by the Regent and all the people of Galicia".[1]

In the following spring the chief purveyor of bread supplied to the fleet at Lisbon, who had mixed lime with the flour, was hanged: and according to a Dublin merchant "in their holy house" in the same city the monks "with great fury" had burned "[the statue of] their holy woman" for appearing to have forsaken them, and there was great "wailing amongst the people".[2]

In Paris, that loquacious old Spanish Ambassador who was going blind, Bernardino de Mendoza, reported that the Queen of England was being extortionately praised by the King of France for having "alone and unaided" trounced the "puissant" Spanish Armada which, he reminded his audience, had taken "four years to gather together". When a courtier dared to remark that "perhaps she was not much afraid of the Duke of Parma" the philosophic King replied, "Time will discover everything".[3]

In England, against the Queen's wishes, the fleet was kept fully manned and vigilant but, although ships and seamen had not made the terrible retreat round the isles that the Spaniards had, ship's fever, or typhus, took its toll of the waiting men so that they sickened and died as they did on the broken Armada.

Helpless, emaciated, half-naked seamen lay dying in the streets of Dover and Rochester as they did at Laredo and Santander.[4]

And there were other similar, seemingly inevitable reactions in the wake of the attempted invasion. "Men muttered that the high command had bungled their business". Drake got the praise which Howard should have received, and Hawkins, "the architect of English victory if any man was"[5] wrote of the "hell" of

[1 & 2] C.S.P.I., pp. 126 and 122.
[3] C.S.P.S., p. 470.
[4 & 5] Mattingly, pp. 314–15.

his infinite "pain and misery" in the endless querulous negotiations over money and payments.

It was rumoured that Raleigh was again to be sent with ships to Ireland; and *Advices from England*, of a gossipy nature which cannot always be trusted but which reflect what was current in a vivid, catching way, reported that:

> The Queen is very much aged and spent, and is very melancholy. Her intimates say that this is caused by the death of the earl of Leicester: but it is very evident that it is rather the fear she underwent and the burden she has upon her.[1]

The writer of the *Advices* did not spare King Philip in his opening when he emphasized the Armada's

> bad management and the heavy loss of [Spanish] ships and men. I will only say that if the Armada had been conducted as it should have been, and its commanders had taken advantage of the opportunities offered to them, the King of Spain would now be as much King of England. . . .

Scrawled in the margin of this manuscript preserved in the Paris Archives, in Philip's own hand, is the comment, "This first is certainly lamentable".

The writer of the *Advices*, Marco Antonio Micea of Genoa, twice stresses the importance of Ireland as a vital pivot in the campaigns beginning to whirl afresh in King Philip's mind:

> This news [of the landing of the Spaniards in Ireland] has caused the Queen and Council much anxiety, as they greatly fear such a war, which they look upon as the most ruinous of any that could happen to them. If there were any means of succouring them [the Spaniards] it would harass the English very much.

To this paragraph the King drew especial attention in his notes. And again, later, the Genoese wrote:

> Now, if the King of Spain wishes to see the Queen of England dead, with the Treasurer, Walsyngham, and all the

[1] C.S.P.S., November 5th, 1588, pp. 479–83.

Council . . . let him send 3-4,000 men to Ireland, and let them fortify themselves there and take the Island. He will soon see the effect. This is the only thing that the English fear; and the real true way to take this country [England] with little risk and trouble; and if a part of the Armada were to effect this they would find it a very different matter to attacking this country [England].

Here Philip scrawled in the margin his customary ejaculation "Ojo!", with the comment "This would be a very important matter".[1]

In Ireland, as early as the end of September 1588, Sir Richard Byngham was writing from his castle at Shrowle, or Shrule, in County Mayo, piously giving thanks, asserting that:

By this may appear the handiwork of Almighty God, who hath drowned the remains of that mighty army, for the most part, on the coasts of this province [Connacht], which was the very place they themselves most doubted [were in fear of], as may appear by the Instructions the Duke of Medina Sidonia gave them after the Queen's ships had left them [in the North Sea].

Enclosing the *Instructions*, which must have been avidly read in England, Byngham went on to assure Fitzwylliam that:

the 700 Spaniards in Ulster [from the two wrecks in Ulster and Donegal] were despatched . . . and this I dare assure your Lordship now, that in a 15 or 16 ships cast away on the coast of this province . . . there hath perished at the least a 6,000 or 7,000 men, of which there hath been put to the sword . . . and executed one way and another, about 700 or 800, or upwards, besides those that yet be alive. . . .

The last set of figures were for Sligo, Mayo, Thomond and Galway alone.

Byngham then adds a paragraph pertinent to loot and what are now called Armada relics:

[1] Ibid., pp. 479-83.

M

Treasure and great wealth hath been taken no doubt, but
that by such unworthy persons, as it will hardly be ever any
thereof come by at all, they be, such as hath it, as before now
have always been, upon their keepings; albeit it is possible in
time some of it may be had.[1]

Sir Edward Denny complained bitterly against the Council's and
Lord Deputy's decision that he must surrender what he had taken,
the loot belonging to Her Majesty the Queen.

It is a curious fact that today few Armada relics are visible or of
easy access. Neither the National Museum of Ireland nor the
British Museum possess any, and many of those described at the
end of the last century or early in this have since disappeared.
One can only presume that they have changed hands privately.
Allingham, writing in 1897, gives drawings of an ornate Spanish
table, and carved chests; and of a wooden figurehead of one
of the ships wrecked with de Cuellar at Streedagh, at that time
in the possession of a Justice of the Peace in Sligo. Today nothing
is known of it locally. Gold rings and chains were taken and
treasured by the Irish people. Brass cannon were lifted for use as
protective ordnance and still adorn some Irish castles, and an
Armada ship's anchor used to be seen at the United Services
Institution in Whitehall. The bell of one ill-fated ship is now used
to ring people to church in Northern Ireland. In 1888 a ter-
centenary Armada Exhibition was held in London, and Allingham lists several chests on show, a Spanish matchlock, a spear-
head, and a spoon

of floral design found near Dunluce Castle and supposed to
come from the wreck of the *Gerona*.

These seem small pickings from the watery end of so many great
ships.

To return to 1588, alarmed by the increasingly dangerous
situation in the north of Ireland, to be wracked by convulsions
almost as violent as geologic upheavals until the Flight of the

[1] C.S.P.I., pp. 48–9.

powerful Earls in 1607, the Privy Council wrote to the Lord Deputy, as it has already been noted, on no account to do battle with the Spaniards reported to be numerous in the north with the added caution:

> We think it meet also that special care should be had of the safe keeping of such prisoners of the Irishry as are in the castle of Dublin lest, getting their liberty, they may join themselves and their followers with the Spaniards. . . .[1]

We know that a handful of Spaniards, eight in number only, who had survived from the wreck of three ships—*La Trinidad Valencera*, the *Juliana* and the *Lavia*—remained in the north, in spite of the fact that all hands were said to have gone down with the two latter ships, until October, 1596, in the service of the great O'Neill and O'Donnell. They humbly sought "wages" from King Philip, through an intermediary, that they might

> fit out their persons and arms the better to serve your Majesty here as guides, interpreters, and otherwsie, as will be needful when the Spanish force lands.[2]

The petition was accompanied by a certificate signed by the two "princes", as the Spaniards elsewhere called them. The *State Papers Spanish* earlier give lists of harbours whose vulnerability and usefulness for the purposes of invasion were weighed in the balance, some in Scotland and England, others in Ireland and Wales, where Milford Haven was cited as being a serviceable harbour. A recently translated Spanish document, dated 1597, lists its advantages, even its two ineffectual pieces of artillery by the entrance tower.

But the danger to England did not prove to come from an alliance of such miserable remnants of fighting Spanish men with the Irish but rather from the Irish themselves, brilliantly led by Tyrone who came within an ace of accomplishing an independent, unified Ireland, only to fail through lack of co-ordination and

[1] Ibid., p. 69.
[2] C.S.P.S., p. 641.

misunderstandings between less far-sighted leaders. The Spaniards, dominated by the paralysing caution and distrust of Philip II, perpetually promised aid and sent nothing but fine letters of pardon for supposed offences against His Majesty, blessings and encouragement, gold chains and portraits of the King. What use were these? When in 1597 some Spanish ships at last arrived in Killybegs harbour the aid they brought proved so paltry that O'Neill, finished once and for all with belief in Spanish promises, broke out with the accusation that "the Spaniards were but a deceitful nation and had cozened the Irish". The ineffectual promises which had elated and beguiled him for so long had resulted in "nothing but a little powder".[1] There followed the Battle of the Yellow Ford, "the greatest defeat inflicted on the English since the thirteenth century", and three years later the annihilation of Essex's troops in a southern pass, where the helmeted heads of the English lay so thickly that it is to this day called the "Pass of the Plumes".

But the end to O'Neill's triumphs came with the Battle of Kinsale, to which southern port, not to Galway in the northwest which O'Neill had urged as wise, the Spaniards again sent ineffectual aid. This was followed by the loss of Dunboy, in the seagirt promontory of Beara in the west, heroically held until the last breath by O'Sullivan Beare's faithful men.

Tyrone, solitary and proud, sought peace at last from a Queen who, without his knowing it, had died six days before. The final fifteen years of her reign had been harassed by constant threats of new Armadas and fresh invasions, of a usurpation of power by the Spaniards allied with the Irish. Out of her straitened budget she had spent more against Tyrone than against any other adversary in her entire reign, more even than in succouring the Protestant Dutch, her aid to them being the second largest sum in her table of extraordinary war expenditure.[2] Now she lay at peace.

[1] C.S.P.S., p. lxii.
[2] *A History of England*, Sir G. M. Trevelyan, pp. 356–7, Financial Table in the Notes.

Along the Irish coasts, in rocky creeks and inlets, the timbers of the Armada ships lay wedged and rotting, festooned with barnacles and green trailing seaweed. One of these, long visible at low tide, when lifted and examined about the turn of the century, proved to be a baulk of Italian oak burnt at the end— one of the frame timbers of the Mediterranean merchantman, *La Rata Encoronada*, burned by de Leyva after she had stranded.

Under the wide curving strands with their white and grey sea-washed sands the bones of de Cuellar's companions, and of other wrecked Armada men on other Irish shores, lay buried to be turned up by the sea or the eroding winds. It is well-known that at Streedagh, when the storms shift the great dunes, quantities of bones may still be washed out. While at *Dun an Oir*, the tragic Fortress of imagined Gold, skulls of the Spanish soldiers are picked up by careless schoolboys and tossed, like so much household rubbish, into the thorny embrace of roadside hedges.

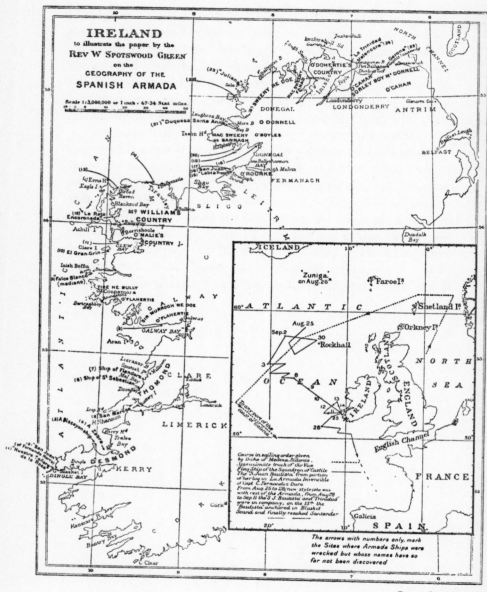

MAP OF THE ARMADA WRECKS by W. Spotswood-Green

NOTE ON THE ILLUSTRATIONS

Frontispiece: SPANISH MARINER'S ASTROLABE, possibly from *Nuestra Señora de la Rosa*. The measurements given by the National Maritime Museum for this rare object are as follows:

Diameter:	7 inches
Thickness at top:	9/16 inches
„ „ bottom:	5/8 inches
Weight:	5½ lbs.

Opposite page 66: ST. MOLAISE. This effigy, of Irish oak and Irish craftsmanship, is of the 13th-14th centuries, but preserves an earlier artistic tradition. It is one of five extant wooden statues in the whole country, and is the only one associated with a saint in the west of Ireland. The figure shows signs of having been painted, and the mutilated face was at some time roughly repaired by the venerating islanders of Inishmurray, whither the effigy was transported from some larger religious building on the mainland, possibly Staad Abbey, Aughros Abbey, or the Dominican House at Sligo. The face is peculiarly Gaelic in caste: long and ascetic it is that of a dedicated man disciplined by fasting. The carving of the hair, which suggests a tonsure, is early Gothic, but the formalized treatment of amice and pointed feet is native. This Irish sculptor's work shows that remote districts of the west were in touch with religious and artistic trends and activities in more populous centres, and it has been described as fit to take its place with the finest work on the continent. (See Catriona Macleod, *Some Wooden Figure Sculptures: Statues of Irish Saints*. Journal of the Royal Society of Antiquaries, Ireland, Vol. LXXXVI, 1946).

Opposite page 83: IRISH KERNES (catharnach), or LIGHT-ARMED NON-PROFESSIONAL SOLDIERS.

A unique English woodcut from the reign of Henry VIII, roughly *c.* 1544–7. Other engravings of Irishmen and women of this date are all by continental artists who had never visited Ireland. Since this was drawn from life it has added significance. For a detailed description of the weapons, headgear and clothing of the figures see H. F. McClintock's *Old Irish and Highland Dress* (Dundalk, 1950, pp. 31–3) in which the author states that this is "the most carefully drawn and authentic of any picture of the period". He draws attention to the "swords with hilts ending in rings . . . through which the tang of the blade passes, a style certainly Irish", and square-fringed scabbards. In spite of their embroidered jackets the men depicted have bare legs and feet and most of them are bare-headed. Their long tunics, drawn up under a belt as in classical times, were clear saffron colour. The woodcut was formerly catalogued as "Irish chieftains", but by the 1580s such men, at least in Ulster, were wearing quilted jackets, mitre-like head-dresses, trews and spurs, possibly due to the influence of the great O'Neill who had been brought up in the houses of Sydney and Leicester and at court in England.

Opposite page 82: ORTELIUS' MAP. From the 1588 edition of his great atlas produced for the Spanish market, with a Spanish text. It had earlier appeared in editions with texts in Latin, French and German, all published at Leiden. Ortelius, born in Antwerp, was Cosmographer to Philip II of Spain and, after Mercator, was the most splendid of all map-makers. It is presumed that the Spanish naval officers sailing with the Armada were familiar with this map. Ortelius, perhaps at Philip's command, had been to Ireland in 1577. It will be seen that he covered the ground thoroughly, far more so than contemporary English map-makers, like Robert Adams. The interior of the country is marked with place-names more correctly spelt than in English maps, and the sea-coasts are prolific in named ports. Furthermore, he gives the lands of the chieftains together with their Gaelic names. But even Ortelius wrongly depicts the north-west coast, ignorance of which caused in part the wreck of so many of the Spanish ships.

Page 176: SPOTSWOOD-GREEN'S MAP OF THE WRECKS. These are not numbered in chronological order. The author and maker-of-the-map emphasized that he pictured the ships forced inshore from the north-west. "Those to the windward would reach Kerry, others Clare, Galway, or Mayo; while the leeward ships, failing to weather the north-west coast of Mayo, would fall away into Donegal Bay" (p. 431). He considered that they arrived in this order and numbered them accordingly. But the State Papers references do not tally with this supposition.

Jacket: Designed from an engraving in the National Maritime Museum by C. J. Visscher, c. 1550–c. 1612, who worked in Amsterdam. By permission of the National Maritime Museum.

Index